Build a Profitable Online Business

The No-Nonsense Guide

Mikael Olsson

Apress·

Build a Profitable Online Business: The No-Nonsense Guide

ISBN-13 (pbk): 978-1-4302-6379-1

ISBN-13 (electronic): 978-1-4302-6380-7

President and Publisher: Paul Manning
Acquisitions Editor: Robert Hutchinson
Editorial Board: Steve Anglin, Mark Beckner, Ewan Buckingham, Gary Cornell, Louise Corrigan, Jonathan Gennick, Jonathan Hassell, Robert Hutchinson, Michelle Lowman, James Markham, Matthew Moodie, Jeff Olson, Jeffrey Pepper, Douglas Pundick, Ben Renow-Clarke, Dominic Shakeshaft, Gwenan Spearing, Matt Wade, Tom Welsh
Coordinating Editor: Rita Fernando
Compositor: SPi Global
Indexer: SPi Global
Cover Designer: Anna Ishchenko

Distributed to the book trade worldwide by Springer Science+Business Media New York, 233 Spring Street, 6th Floor, New York, NY 10013. Phone 1-800-SPRINGER, fax (201) 348-4505, e-mail orders-ny@springer-sbm.com, or visit www.springeronline.com. Apress Media, LLC is a California LLC and the sole member (owner) is Springer Science + Business Media Finance Inc (SSBM Finance Inc). SSBM Finance Inc is a **Delaware** corporation.

For information on translations, please e-mail rights@apress.com, or visit www.apress.com.

Apress and friends of ED books may be purchased in bulk for academic, corporate, or promotional use. eBook versions and licenses are also available for most titles. For more information, reference our Special Bulk Sales–eBook Licensing web page at www.apress.com/bulk-sales.

Any source code or other supplementary materials referenced by the author in this text is available to readers at www.apress.com. For detailed information about how to locate your book's source code, go to www.apress.com/source-code/.

Contents at a Glance

Contents

About the Author

Mikael Olsson is a professional web entrepreneur, programmer, and author. He works for an R&D company in Finland where he specializes in software development. In his spare time he writes books and creates websites that summarize various fields of interest. The books he writes are focused on teaching their subject in the most efficient way possible, by explaining only what is relevant and practical without any unnecessary repetition or theory. The portal to his online businesses and other websites is Siforia.com.

Preface

This is a concise handbook for creating and running a successful web business. It will teach you the essentials of how to earn money online through a website. It is primarily intended for individuals who want to generate passive income by leveraging the Internet with a limited amount of time and money. Nonetheless, most of the strategies set out in this book apply equally well to companies and other organizations.

This is a practical hands-on book that will take you step by step through the process of establishing and promoting a money-generating website. Just as the advice in this book is framed to serve the needs of web entrepreneurs with limited time and money, this book's presentation is itself stripped down for speed and action. Whether you are new to online business or already have websites running, you will benefit from this condensation of the information I have gathered from thousands of hours of study and practice. To get the most out of the material, read this book first from beginning to end, and then read it again section by section as you go along, applying its no-nonsense business strategies and technical advice to building your own profitable online business.

Let's begin.

PART 1

Site Setup

CHAPTER 1

Site Type and Niche

Before creating a website you need to decide on two things: what type of site it will be, and what niche you will be focusing on.

Site Type

The site type defines the main kind of value your site will offer to visitors. There are three broad categories:

- **Informational site** – Teaches, informs, guides, and keeps visitors up to date.

- **Entertainment site** – Entertains visitors through blog, stories, or multimedia.

- **E-commerce site** – Provides a service or sells a product.

No one type is necessarily easier to build or more profitable than another. An *entertainment site* typically has the easiest time attracting visitors, yet it earns the least per visitor. Conversely, an *e-commerce site* generally has the hardest time attracting visitors, yet it earns the most per visitor. *Information sites* tend to fall somewhere in between the other two in terms of traffic and earnings.

I recommend that you choose a site type according to your own strengths and resources. If you own exclusive rights to a product, then an e-commerce site selling that product would be the obvious choice. Similarly, if you are an expert at a subject, then teaching it through an informational site would be a good idea. Lastly, if humor or multimedia is your strong point, then an entertainment site may be your best starting point.

Content and E-Commerce Sites

To simplify things, informational and entertainment sites will be lumped together as *content sites* in this book. Whichever site type you choose—content or e-commerce—you are not bound to stick only to that type. That is only your starting point. For your site to become both popular and profitable, it is generally required that you start with one type and then combine it with the other type. You may start off with an e-commerce site and then expand into a content site to attract more traffic. Or else you may start with a content site and add aspects of an e-commerce site in order to generate more revenue from your traffic. Such a combined site will be referred to as a *content/e-commerce* site.

Site Niche

In addition to choosing what type of site to start with, you also need to choose a niche for your site. The *niche* specifies in one phrase what your site will be about. It can be a general niche—such as *golf*—or a more specific niche—such as *golf clubs*. Either way, your site must not deviate from the niche you decide on. Consistent branding is a key aspect of developing a popular and profitable site, because sharp niche focus will make it easier to rank highly in search engines and thus attract a greater flow of visitors, so vital to monetizing your site. If you keep that focus, visitors will begin to think of your site as *the* place to go to find out about things in your niche.

Niche Interest

There are a virtually unlimited number of topical niches for you to choose from. Rather than choosing the most popular and profitable one you can find, I recommend that you pick a niche reflects your own interests and passions. If you select a niche that is interesting and enjoyable to you, you will stand a much greater chance of being successful at it. Do not let your new career as a web entrepreneur become another boring job. Shape it instead into a profitable hobby.

Niche Popularity

No matter how keen your personal interest in a particular niche, you must also realistically assess the popularity of the niche. This will determine the upper limits of how much traffic your site can potentially attract and therefore, to a large degree, how much money you can expect to earn from it. The easiest way to determine the popularity of a niche is to use the Google AdWords Keyword Planner.[*] This tool quantifies the global monthly searches on Google for any term you specify. A niche whose keywords elicit fewer than 10,000 broad monthly searches is a dubious web business prospect.

In addition to the Google AdWords Keyword Planner, you can use Google Trends[†] to discover if a niche is rising or falling in popularity. This Google tool displays a graph showing how the worldwide search volume for a given keyword phrase has changed over time. A niche with a positive trend is preferable, though the monthly search volume is a more important factor.

---

[*]https://adwords.google.com/ko/KeywordPlanner
[†]http://www.google.com/trends

Niche Competition

When you have found a niche that is both interesting and popular, the third step is to consider the competition. To estimate this you can use the Keyword Efficiency Index (KEI) formula:

$$\frac{(monthly\ searches)^2}{competing\ sites}$$

You can find out the number of competing sites by searching for the niche on Google in quotation marks. The number of search results returned will be the number of competing sites. For example, a niche with 10,000 monthly searches and 1,000,000 competing sites would have a KEI of $[(10^4)^2/10^6] = 100$. An index above 10 is considered good and above 100 is excellent. The higher KEI value the niche has, the less crowded the niche will be, and the easier it will be to grow your site's traffic levels.

.

CHAPTER 2

Web Hosting

In order to have a website that is accessible on the Internet at all times, there are two separate things you need to do. First, you need to register a domain name, and second you need to find a server to host your website.

You can register your domain at one place and host it somewhere else, though most web hosts offer domain registration as well. The factors to consider when selecting a web host are: *reliability*, *performance*, *bandwidth constraints*, *web space*, *price*, and the *peripheral services* that are offered.

Reliability

A site that is frequently down will lose visitors and search ranking. Ideally, look for a minimum uptime guarantee of 99.5% or higher. The web host should provide some form of refund if it falls below its promise.

Performance

The server speed is an important factor to consider. A slow site will appear less professional to visitors, which reduces its credibility and thereby its conversion rates. It will also lower the site's quality score in Google, and your search rankings will suffer as a result. However, a slow site is often not the result of a slow server, but of other factors relating to the site itself and its content. These issues will be discussed in the chapter on Performance.

There are two basic types of web hosting packages: shared and dedicated. On a *shared host* a server is shared by many webmasters, whereas on a *dedicated host* you have the server and all of its resources to yourself. The dedicated type offers faster response time with high traffic loads and greater control. However, the shared host type is much cheaper, so I recommend you to use that type when you start out. A dedicated server will not ever be needed for most sites, though you may want to look into it if your site reaches more than 10,000 visitors per day. A transfer may become necessary with fewer visitors if your site serves dynamic rather than static content.

If you plan to offer file downloads or media streaming through your website, these should not be hosted on the same server that hosts your site. You want the performance of your site to be unaffected by the number of people who use such bandwidth-intensive services.

Bandwidth

Contrary to many web hosts' claims, there are no hosts actually offering "unlimited bandwidth." Bandwidth is cheap, but not free. Always look for details as to how much traffic the package allows, and whether you are allowed to purchase more bandwidth at a later time.

Web Space

Does the host offer enough space for your needs? Just as for bandwidth, do not accept the term "unlimited" at face value. Read the package descriptions carefully. Usually, "unlimited" will be redefined to be limited in some way.

Price

Shared web hosting is cheap. You may pay more for coffee in a day than the monthly fee for your web host. Because of this, the price should not be your main concern when choosing a web host. The other factors play a much more important role in building a profitable online business.

Other Services

Check which services are included and which ones cost extra. Here are some important services to look for.

- **PHP and MySQL** – Vital for most sites. PHP allows your site to offer dynamic content and MySQL is a database management system.

- **Technical support** – Very important. When something goes wrong with the server, you want someone competent to fix it.

- **FTP and SSH access** – Important. Makes it easy to transfer files to and from your server.

- **Daily backups** – Useful. You can set up this yourself, but it is nice if the web host includes it for free.

- **Dedicated IP** – Often not important. One reason to have it would be to make sure your search rankings are unaffected by the actions of other webmasters on your shared host.

Do not pay extra for services you are not certain you will need. Many web hosts will attempt to sell you a lot of needless services while you are in the process of signing up for them. Also, be sure to search for vouchers to the host you plan to subscribe to, since these can significantly improve the deal you get.

Recommended Hosts

Take your time and select the host that best meets your needs. It will be well worth the effort in the long run. Some high-quality hosting companies where you might start your search include:

- **DreamHost** – www.dreamhost.com
- **MediaTemple** – www.mediatemple.net
- **GoDaddy** – www.godaddy.com
- **A Small Orange** – www.asmallorange.com
- **Webfaction** – www.webfaction.com

CHAPTER 3

Domain Name

Choosing and registering your domain name is an initial step in creating your online business that should not be taken lightly, because a careless choice can undermine your business prospects before you even begin.

Choosing a Proper Domain Name

Your domain name is your Internet identity—your online brand name. For any online business the importance of choosing a proper domain name cannot be overstated. Your domain name should have the following characteristics:

- **Primary keywords** – Including your site's primary keyword(s) in the domain name is often a good idea. This will give a significant boost to your search engine rankings for those terms.

- **Easy to remember** – Get a catchy domain name that is easy to say, type, and remember. It will help people spread the word about your site more easily.

A domain name can have up to 63 characters. It can contain any combination of letters and numbers, as well as hyphens and underscores.

Domain Age

The age of the domain name is one of the many factors that Google considers when ranking a site. An old domain shows permanence and therefore gives a higher quality score in Google. Because of this, you may want to consider registering domain names even before you are sure you are going to need them.

The active age of a domain starts from the time the search engines find the site, not from when you register it. Therefore, you should create an initial link to each domain name you register from a web page that is already indexed by the search engines. The search engine's web crawlers will then follow the link and learn of the existence of your new domain. This is a more efficient approach than submitting your domain name to all search engines in order to be included.

Registration Period

Make sure you register your domain for the longest amount of time possible. Register for five years or more if you can. This is especially important for new sites. Search engines—particularly Google—look at the length of your domain's registration as a quality factor for your site. They do this because many spam sites have short registrations, and a longer registration period indicates that you are building a site with long-term value.

Domain Extension

When registering a new domain name for a commercial website, you want to get the .com domain extension. It is the most popular extension and is therefore the easiest one to remember. It is also the default extension people will try if they type in your domain name by hand. One possible exception is if you are only serving a local market. In that case a country specific extension will make your site rank slightly higher for searches coming from that country.

Finding Available Domain Names

An incredible number of names are already registered and more are registered every day. Therefore, finding a good domain name that is available—especially a .com one—can be very difficult. Below are two domain suggestion tools that make this process a whole lot simpler. Simply type in your keywords and see what domain names related to those terms are currently available.

- DomainTools – `domain-suggestions.domaintools.com`
- DomainIt – `www.domainit.com/domain-suggest-tool.mhtml`

If the name you want is registered you may be able to purchase it from a domain name brokering company, such as Sedo.[*]

Registering a Domain Name

To register a domain name, you need to use an accredited domain name registrar or one of their agents. Often, your web hosting company has a relationship with a particular registrar that allows you to purchase your web hosting account and domain name with one transaction. That is easy, but it is not always the cheapest option.

---

[*] `http://www.sedo.com`

CHAPTER 4

Site Structure

Content Management Systems

For most people, building your site from scratch is a really bad idea. Even if you have the technical know-how, it would be a waste of time since there are already so many great *Content Management Systems* (CMSs) out there. A CMS is a tool that helps you manage the creation and updating of your website. Such a tool uses databases and web programming languages, such as PHP, to give you a dynamic site. With a dynamic site your pages are generated dynamically, and so there is no need to have any static HTML files on your server. A CMS site basically consists of the following elements:

- **Template** – A handful of template files describing the site's structure and design.

- **Style** – A CSS style sheet describing the site's style information.

- **Database** – A database containing the web pages' text content, among many other things.

- **Components** – Images and other static components used by your site.

WordPress

The one CMS I would recommend above all others is WordPress (WP).[*] Although initially created specifically for building blogs, WordPress has since evolved into a powerful CMS capable of running just about any type of site. It is built with PHP and is both free and open source. Some more reasons for choosing WP include:

- **Easy to use** – Updating your site is simple. You do not even need to know HTML.

- **Customizable** – A huge community of developers is constantly creating free themes and plug-ins that you can use to customize your site.

---

[*]http://wordpress.org

- **Support** – Because of its popularity, finding support and getting help is very easy.

- **SEO** – WordPress makes it easy to apply the many search engine optimization techniques that will be discussed in Part 2.

The WordPress Codex[†] contains the official documentation for WordPress. It is well organized and lets you easily find anything you need to know about WP. Some important pages you may want to look through in the WP Codex include:

- **Installing WordPress** – codex.wordpress.org/Installing_WordPress

- **Administrating your site** – codex.wordpress.org/Administering_Your_Blog

- **Using themes** – codex.wordpress.org/Using_Themes

- **Theme development** – codex.wordpress.org/Theme_Development

- **Managing plug-ins** – codex.wordpress.org/Managing_Plugins

Site Pages

In terms of an online business website, you can categorize your web pages into four categories:

- **Content pages** – Their purpose is to attract visitors to your site and to keep them there.

- **Navigation pages** – Pages containing mainly links to other internal pages.

- **Sales pages** – Product or service selling pages aimed at converting visitors into customers.

- **Credibility pages** – Pages whose main purpose is to boost the site's credibility and thereby achieve higher conversion rates.

Each of these will be covered in detail in later chapters. Generally, you want your site to include all of these page types, irrespective of whether you have a content site or an e-commerce site.

An e-commerce site is focused on sales pages. However, it can be supplemented with content pages, because these are easier to market and help drive traffic to the site. Additionally, content pages lend your site more credibility and authority as well as help build your brand.

Similarly, a content site can add sales pages to increase its revenue. This helps the site capitalize on its traffic, which is often much greater than that of an e-commerce site.

[†]http://codex.wordpress.org

CHAPTER 5

Site Design

Template

Once your CMS is installed on your web server, the next task is to design your website's template, also called *theme*. Instead of attempting to improve upon the default template, my advice is that you find a professional-looking template that closely fits your purposes, and then modify it according to your visitors' needs. This will simplify your design work immensely. If WordPress is your CMS of choice, then you can find a quality template at WordPress's own theme directory.[*]

Even with a well-designed template as your starting point, a significant amount of work and technical know-how is required to create a template that stands out while at the same time being everything your visitors need. I recommend that you invest some time in learning the skills of a web programmer—namely, HTML,[†] CSS,[‡] JavaScript,[§] and PHP.[‖] Knowing these languages will allow you to modify your site's template yourself. Alternatively, you can delegate this whole task to a professional web designer and developer. Either way, be sure to design your site from the visitors' perspective more than from your own.

What Makes a Good Web Design

A professional web design is one that is both elegant and has a high usability. It needs to be attractive to look at while at the same time helping visitors to find what they are looking for: the content, product, or service. It is essential to maximize both qualities. Anything less than a professional design will make your site seem small and unreliable.

---

[*]http://wordpress.org/themes/
[†]http://www.pvtuts.com/html/
[‡]http://www.pvtuts.com/css/
[§]http://www.pvtuts.com/javascript/
[‖]http://www.pvtuts.com/php/

Elegance

An elegant design is one where the page elements are balanced, flow well together, and have matching style, color and lines. This elegance translates into credibility and will make your site more likeable. Some generic design guidelines to follow include:

- **Font** – Use an easy-to-read font such as Verdana, Arial, or Times in a standard size.

- **Colors** – Usually, two main colors from which you can go with several nuances are enough. The two colors should be similar and not be too subtle or vibrant.

- **Background** – Avoid the temptation to add a background image. In general, background images are a distraction for the visitor. A solid color background matching your site's color theme appears more professional and lends your site more credibility.

- **Background color** – For readability's sake, the background should be bright and the text black.

- **Whitespace** – Whitespace is essential to keep the layout from appearing cluttered.

We all know good design when we see it. Therefore, I am not going to bore you too much with design theory. Instead, I advise you to gather inspiration from well-designed sites, such as the majority of the largest sites on the web.*

Layout

Most successful websites have very similar layouts. Usually, they are made up of two or three columns: a wider content column and one or two navigational columns. The main navigation menu is in the left column or horizontally across the top of the page. The content is in the wider middle column as the focal point of the page. Sub-navigation and additional reading related to the content is in the right column. The site or company logo appears at the top left or center of the header, and at the bottom of the page is a footer showing where the web page ends.

The design needs to have balance in its layout. What this means is that the elements need to be balanced across either side of the centerline, so that the design appears even. For example, a large element on the right side may be balanced by a similar element on the left. It can also be balanced through several smaller elements on the left or by placing one smaller element further out to the left.

You may want to organize and balance the page elements offline first, as simple boxes in a grid system, before you modify your site template accordingly.

---

*http://www.alexa.com/topsites/

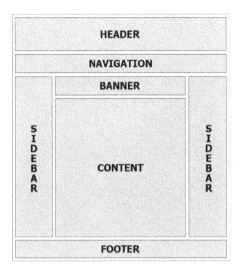

Example of a layout grid

Usability

Usability represents the ease of use inherent in your site's design, navigation, and functionality. The idea behind the practice is to make your site so intuitive that the visitor can use it without expending any effort thinking about how to use it.

Following standards that web users are already familiar with improves the usability of your site—for example, having a left side navigational menu. Another important usability guideline is to have a consistent look and feel on each page.

CHAPTER 6

Performance

Making sure that your visitors can view your site as fast as possible is of vital importance to any website. It not only affects the average time a user stays on your site and their return rate, but also your site's perceived credibility. All of these factors influence the revenue your site can generate. A fast site not only gives a better user experience, but also appears more professional and of a higher quality. Page respond time and load time are also two of the quality factors that influence your Google search ranking.

Analyzing Site Performance

Before you start to optimize your site, you need a way to measure your site's current performance so that you can quantify any improvements. A convenient way to get this information is to run your site through Pingdom's Full page test.* This tool does a quick visual benchmark of the load time of all components on your site. It gives you a grasp of which components you may need to optimize. Be sure to save the information for later reference.

An example of a Pingdom benchmark

---

*http://tools.pingdom.com/fpt/

Note that, in terms of user experience, reducing the page load time should not be your main concern. Of greater importance is the time it takes until the visitor is able to access and interact with the page.

A less graphical but more detailed report on your site performance can be obtained using the Web Page Analyzer.[*] This is an excellent tool that analyzes a webpage and gives recommendations for decreasing its load time.

YSlow

The following two Firefox plug-ins will be of immense help as you optimize your site.

■ **Note** Firebug[†] – Provides debugging abilities for Firefox.

YSlow[‡] – Integrates with Firebug to add performance analyzing functionality.

With these plug-ins installed, navigate to the page you want to analyze. Next, click on the YSlow icon on the status bar to bring up the YSlow tab of the Firebug window.

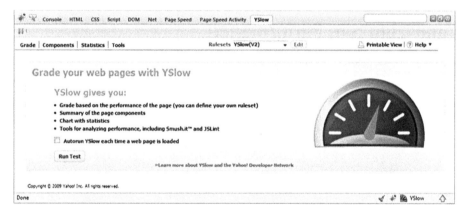

YSlow start screen

From there, click the Run Test button to make an instant performance analysis of your website. This will show you where your site is slow and what you can do to improve it.

Look through all of the performance categories, even the ones you already have an "A" grade in, to learn in what areas you may be able to optimize. For each category there is a link to Yahoo's Performance Rules[§] that further describes how you may implement the optimizations.

---

[*]http://www.websiteoptimization.com/services/analyze/
[†]http://www.getfirebug.com/
[‡]http://developer.yahoo.com/yslow/
[§]http://developer.yahoo.com/performance/rules.html

YSlow will give your site an overall performance score from 0-100. It is recommended that you bring your site up to at least 80.

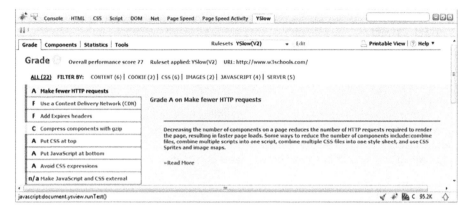

YSlow grade tab

YSlow includes three more tabs—components, statistics and tools—that you should examine as well. In particular, the statistics tab can provide some useful data.

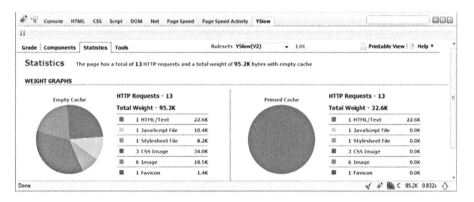

YSlow statistics tab

For more information about YSlow, take a look at the YSlow user guide.* Another Firebug extension similar to YSlow is Google's Page Speed plug-in. It will give you Google's perspective on what makes a high performance website and is definitely worth testing out.

---

*http://yslow.org/user-guide/

■ **Note**   Page Speed* – Adds performance analyzing functionality to Firebug, similar to YSlow.

Page Size

Reducing the size of the XHTML document that makes up a web page can significantly improve a page's load time. As seen in your Pingdom benchmark, the XHTML document needs to be fully downloaded before the browser can start downloading the other components.

A good guideline is that the page size, excluding the components, should not be more than 50kb if possible. To reduce the size of all your pages, you can try to shave off redundant HTML elements from within your CMS template code. You may also want to split content across multiple pages for very large documents.

W3 Total Cache

One of the best techniques for speeding up a WordPress site is to install the W3 Total Cache plug-in. While there are a great many plug-ins related to WordPress performance, this is the only one you really need. It includes page caching, database caching, minification, http compression, and transparent CDN integration—each of which will be explained later in this chapter.

■ **Note**   W3 Total Cache† – This WP plug-in improves overall site performance.

With this plug-in fully configured and running, there are few remaining optimizations you need to make for your site. Techniques such as reducing the total number of database queries and executed PHP code become unnecessary when you are providing static cached pages to the visitors.

Page Caching

Most CMSs—including WordPress—run on PHP, which is an interpreted programming language. This means that, any time a visitor arrives at such a site, the server has to compile the requested PHP files, execute database queries, and finally send the compiled HTML file to the end user. Because of this, commonly mentioned optimization techniques for WordPress sites include:

- Replacing PHP code with static HTML.
- Reducing the number of database queries.
- Removing or disabling plug-ins.

---

*http://code.google.com/speed/page-speed/
†http://wordpress.org/plugins/w3-total-cache/

While such changes can significantly improve performance on an uncached WordPress site, they have no effect on a site cached with, for example, W3 Total Cache. On such a site visitors will instead be served precompiled cached HTML files. It is in fact preferable to keep your WordPress template files dynamic with PHP and database queries, in order to make the site easier to modify. You then get the best of both worlds: the speed of static HTML files and the modifiability of dynamic PHP.

Content Delivery Network

A *Content Delivery Network* or CDN allows you to host your static files on a subdomain which is linked to a wide network of servers all over the world. This means that your static content—such as HTML, cached PHP, images, JavaScript and CSS—is pushed to a server that is closer to the intended recipient, making it load much faster. This will greatly reduce bandwidth consumption and the number of HTTP requests issued to your web server, although at a financial cost.

CDN service providers include, for example, Amazon Cloudfront, Akamai Technologies, Mirror Image Internet, and Limelight Networks. Their services are not free, but as your number of visitors grow larger, a CDN becomes necessary to achieve fast response times.

Cache-Control Header

A *cache-control header* tells the browser how long it should keep content in its cache. This can be used to reduce the page load time and number of HTTP requests for second time visitors. In particular, you want to cache static components that you are unlikely to change—not only images, but also JavaScript files, CSS files, and Flash components.

This optimization is performed automatically by W3 Total Cache and it can be configured under the Browser Cache Settings page. Keep in mind that if you use a far future expiration date you normally have to change the component's filename whenever it is modified in order to ensure consistency across all visitors. With W3 Total Cache installed, however, this will be done automatically for you whenever you update a cached component.

Compressing Components

Enabling gzip compression is a simple and effective way to save bandwidth and speed up your site. W3 Total Cache will enable gzip for text-based components automatically. Most images, music, and videos should not be gzipped, because they are already compressed. Only text is worth compressing—with CSS, JavaScript and HTML being the most important text files. Only browsers supporting compression will be sent compressed components, making this technique compatible with older browsers.

The tradeoff with gzipping components is an increased server CPU-load. Usually, this is a good tradeoff, given the speed of compression. It is also possible to store gzipped static components and to send over the pre-compressed versions. This is done by default by W3 Total Cache for cached text-based files.

Minimize HTTP Requests

One of the largest factors influencing the page load time is the number of components that are present on that page. Components include everything that requires an extra HTTP request, after the page has been fetched when the visitor's cache is empty.

Examples of components include images, videos, style sheets, scripts, and Flash. There is an inherent overhead in each HTTP request. Therefore, reducing the number of separate components required to render a page will improve its performance for first-time visitors.

Split Components across Domains

In order to maximize the number of active download threads, the components can be split across multiple domains. However, because there is a penalty for the DNS to map an IP address from a given hostname, using a separate domain for every component is not a good idea either. It is recommended to use at least two but no more than four domains for optimal performance. This gives a good compromise between reducing DNS lookups and increasing the number of parallel downloads.

Preload Components

By preloading components you can take advantage of the time the browser is idle and request components that the visitor is likely to need in the future. This way, when the user visits the next page, you could have most of the components already in the cache and thereby allow the page to load much faster.

Preloading components typically involves writing JavaScript code that executes after the onload event. An example of such script prefetching that works across many browsers can be found on `phpied.com`.*

Link Prefetching

Another way of preloading components is by using the HTML <link> tag. This tag, when added to a page, provides a set of prefetching hints to the browser. After the browser is finished loading the page and is idle, it will begin silently prefetching the specified documents and storing them in its cache. This link prefetching is currently only supported by Firefox. However, since Firefox is the second most popular web browser, you can noticeably decrease load times for a large percentage of your visitors just by adding one line of code to your HTML markup. For prefetching purposes, the Firefox browser looks for an HTML <link> tag with a relation type of either "next" or "prefetch." An example of using the <link> tag to prefetch a web page would look like this:

```
<link rel="next" href="nextpage.php" />
```

---

*`http://www.phpied.com/preload-cssjavascript-without-execution/`

24

Link prefetching can also be used for static components, such as images.

```
<link rel="prefetch" href="image.jpg" />
```

WordPress sites include a link tag by default to prefetch the next post.

Post-Load Components

The onload event can, in addition to preloading, also be used to post-load components, although this is less common. For example, large images below the fold can be loaded after the rest of the components have finished loading. This can be achieved by using the YUI Image Loader* utility, which is part of the YUI JavaScript library. Similarly, there is the YUI Get Utility,† which lets you include JS and CSS after the page has loaded.

Cookie-Free Domains

When the browser makes a request for a static component on a domain that uses cookies, the server will send those cookies along with the request. This creates needless network traffic. Therefore, static components should be hosted on a domain or subdomain different from your website's domain. This can be achieved, for example, by using a CDN.

CSS and JavaScript

CSS Sprites

CSS sprites are the preferred method for reducing the number of HTTP requests for images. A sprite is an image made up of several smaller images. Using the CSS background-image and background-position properties, you can display the desired image segment from this sprite. For more information you can read about CSS sprites on CSS-Tricks.com.‡

Make JavaScript and CSS External and Single File

Using external code files generally produces faster pages than inlining the code on the web page, although they require separate HTTP requests. This is because external code files—such as JavaScript and CSS files—are cached by the browser. Therefore, the size of the HTML document is reduced without increasing the number of HTTP requests for second-time visitors.

In order to minimize the number of HTTP requests, make sure to put your JavaScript into a single file. Likewise, be sure to place all CSS rules in a single style sheet document. The exception to this is when you have a page that only has one page view per session. In this case, you may find that inlining the code will result in faster load times.

---

*http://developer.yahoo.com/yui/imageloader/
†http://developer.yahoo.com/yui/get/
‡http://css-tricks.com/css-sprites/

CSS on Top

Placing your site's style sheet within the <head> element of the document makes pages appear to load faster. This is because it allows the browser to render the page progressively. The browser will display whatever content it has as soon as it can, which gives the visitor visual feedback and improves the overall user experience.

JavaScript on Bottom

JavaScript files should be placed on the bottom of the page whenever possible. This is because scripts block parallel downloads for all but the latest browsers: IE8+, Firefox 3.5+, Chrome 2+, and Safari 4+. In some situations, it is not easy to move scripts to the bottom. For example, if the script uses document.write to insert part of the page's content, it cannot be moved lower on the page.

Minify JavaScript and CSS

Minification is the practice of removing unnecessary characters from code to reduce its size. When code is minified, all whitespace characters are removed and the code is optimized and restructured so as to load faster. To compress CSS, you can use an online tool, such as CleanCSS.* Compressing JavaScript can be done with, for example, the JavaScript Compressor.† Note that W3 Total Cache will do these optimizations for you, so if you have that plug-in installed you do not need to manually minify your code.

One optimization that minification tools are unable to do is to find and remove unused CSS rules. A useful Firefox plug-in that can help you perform this task is Dust-Me Selectors. This plug-in can both test pages individually and scan through an entire site in search of unused selectors.

■ **Note**   Dust-Me Selectors‡ – A Firefox plug-in that finds unused CSS selectors.

Reducing Download Iterations

When a visitor arrives at your site, their browser will first download the initial HTML web page. Once that page has been received any external components referenced from that page will begin downloading, such as JavaScript and CSS files. If these components in turn contain external components these will have to be downloaded in a third iteration since the browser will not know about them until the first external component has been loaded. This can be seen in the following Pingdom benchmark.

---

*http://www.cleancss.com
†http://javascriptcompressor.com
‡http://www.sitepoint.com/dustmeselectors/

Load time in seconds	URL	Size(KB)
1	www.programmingvideotutorials.com/	14.2
2	...als.com/wp-content/w3tc/min/570aa4/default.include.4075883070.css	12.3
3	d3gzmfcxsyv953.cloudfront.net/images/pvt-banner.png	18.6
4	d3gzmfcxsyv953.cloudfront.net/images/donate.gif	2.7
5	d3gzmfcxsyv953.cloudfront.net/images/hos.png	8.4
6	d3gzmfcxsyv953.cloudfront.net/images/pwm.png	6.1
7	d3gzmfcxsyv953.cloudfront.net/js/scripts.js	24.9
8	d3gzmfcxsyv953.cloudfront.net/images/bg.png	3.2
9	d3gzmfcxsyv953.cloudfront.net/images/icons.png	6.5
10	d3gzmfcxsyv953.cloudfront.net/images/bg-vertical.png	0.1
11	d3gzmfcxsyv953.cloudfront.net/images/bg-content.png	0.2

0   0.2   0.4   0.6   0.8   1   1.2   1.4   1.6   1.8 s

A page requiring three download iterations

By removing the third download iteration, the first page view will load faster. Embedding all JavaScript in a single script file, and all CSS rules in a single style sheet file, will remove some of the need for the third download iteration. What you must also do is to begin downloading any images used in the CSS file as soon as the web page has loaded. This is done by referencing the images from an internal style sheet on the web page using the CSS background property.[*] The example below shows a CSS rule that references two images to be prefetched.

```
<style type="text/css">
#preload {
  background:url( img1.png ) no-repeat -9999px -9999px;
  background:url( img2.png ) no-repeat -9999px -9999px;
}
</style>
```

Web browsers will not begin fetching a CSS background image until they know for sure that it will be used. Therefore, you need to actually use the CSS rule in the document for this optimization to work. This is the reason why the prefetched images are hidden from view by being moved off the screen. In the code above, the id selector[†] is used, so by applying that selector to the body tag, the images will be prefetched.

```
<body id="preload">
```

With this optimization in place, the page previously benchmarked will be able to load in only two download iterations.

---

[*]http://www.pvtuts.com/css/css-background
[†]http://www.pvtuts.com/css/css-class-id-selectors

Load time in seconds	URL	Size(KB)
1	www.programmingvideotutorials.com/	14.6
2	...als.com/wp-content/w3tc/min/570aa4/default.include.4075883070.css	12.3
3	d3qzmfcxsyv953.cloudfront.net/images/bg.png	3.2
4	d3qzmfcxsyv953.cloudfront.net/images/icons.png	6.6
5	d3qzmfcxsyv953.cloudfront.net/images/bg-vertical.png	0.1
6	d3qzmfcxsyv953.cloudfront.net/images/bg-content.png	0.2
7	d3qzmfcxsyv953.cloudfront.net/images/pvt-banner.png	18.6
8	d3qzmfcxsyv953.cloudfront.net/images/donate.gif	2.7
9	d3qzmfcxsyv953.cloudfront.net/images/hos.png	8.4
10	d3qzmfcxsyv953.cloudfront.net/images/pwm.png	6.1
11	d3qzmfcxsyv953.cloudfront.net/js/script.js	25.3

0   0.2   0.4   0.6   0.8   1   1.2   1.4   1.6   1.8 s

Same page as before, but now requiring only two download iterations

Image Optimization

Graphics and photos often constitute a significant amount of the page size, so optimizing them should be a high priority. The three image formats supported by all browsers are jpg, gif, and png. These formats have the following properties:

	PNG	JPG	GIF
Compression	Lossless zip compression	Lossy compression, Adjustable quality/size	Lossless compression
Transparency	Variable transparency	No transparency	Single level transparency
Colors	Variable bit depth8, 24 or 48 bits	Always 24 bit	Up to 256 colors only
Progressive display	Two-dimensional interlacing	Progressive display	One-dimensional interlacing

For photographic images (continuous tones), the jpg format produces the smallest file size. When saving the file, you can also reduce the size further by selecting a lower quality. For graphics (solid color images), the png format gives file sizes smaller than jpg and in most cases smaller than gif. Basically, png is an excellent substitute for gif that was built to handle the same types of graphics better and faster.

Another important aspect to image optimization is the image dimensions. Typically, you should not scale the width and height of an image down in HTML. This makes the image appear jagged and gives an unnecessarily large download size for the end user. However, it is recommended to include the width and height attributes of the <img> element, in order to state the image's actual dimensions. This allows the browser to reserve space for the image and to render it faster once it has finished downloading.

To make an image appear to load faster, it can be saved as either "interlaced" (gif/png) or with "progressive loading" (jpg) format. Browsers will then start to draw the image before it is fully loaded. This improves the user experience at the cost of a slightly larger file size. It is most useful for large images that appear above the fold.

A final optimizing technique is to remove unnecessary bytes without changing the visual quality of the image. A useful online tool for this purpose is Smushit.*

Compare Results

Are you satisfied with your optimizations? Then it is time to test your site. See if it can outperform your competitors' sites with Pingdom.† You can also sign up for a free account with Pingdom to be able to monitor the page response time from various locations around the world.

---

[18]http://www.smushit.com/ysmush.it
[19]http://tools.pingdom.com

CHAPTER 7

Validation

Once your site is implemented, designed, and optimized, it is time for validation and usability testing. This provides a means of correcting any problems before revealing your site to the general public. There are several ways to validate your website. Most importantly, you should validate your HTML, CSS, and SEO, as well as ensure that you have no broken links or images.

Code Validation

The following validation tests can be used to make sure your website code does not contain any errors.

- **HTML validation** – The W3C Markup Validation Service will list any markup errors found on a submitted page. Another similar tool is the WDG HTML Validator, which can check every page on your site.

- **CSS validation** – The W3C CSS Validation Service can validate your CSS to ensure the style information behind your pages is clean and valid.

- **Link validation** – The W3C Link Checker makes sure that you do not have any broken links.

SEO Validation

A SEO validator is a service that lets you test your website against search engine ranking factors. There are a number of online tools available for this purpose. Below are two of the better ones.

- **IBeam's SEO Site Validator** – This tool will go through a couple of pages on your site and give you a SEO score and title.

- **SEO Workers Analysis Tool** – An advanced and somewhat verbose tool that tries to analyze a page from a search crawler's perspective.

Accessibility Validation

Web accessibility means making your website usable by people with disabilities. To help evaluate if your site is accessible, you can use Wave,* which is a free web accessibility evaluation tool.

Browser Compatibility Testing

Make sure your website looks the same on all of the major browsers—namely Firefox, Internet Explorer, Chrome, Safari, and Opera. These web browsers together make up about 99% of the market share, as seen below.

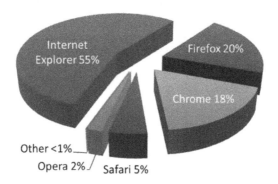

Browser market share. Source: NetMarketShare.com, 2013

A useful tool for checking browser compatibility is BrowserShots.† It will show you how your site will look on different versions of the browsers you select. Web pages may render slightly differently on older versions of the same browser, even if your markup is correct. For this reason, it is important to test previous versions since many web users are still using them.

To make your website render correctly for around 99% of the Internet population, you should test compatibility for browser versions down to IE6, Firefox 3.0, Chrome 5.0, Safari 4.0, and Opera 10.0. Additionally, you may want to test out your site on mobile web browsers, for example using mobiReady.‡ Making your site easily accessible through mobile devices is becoming more and more important. You may want to consider using a separate lightweight template specifically for your mobile visitors.

▩   WP Mobile Detector§ – This plug-in detects mobile devices and displays a compatible WordPress mobile theme.

You also want to make sure that your site looks good at lower monitor resolutions, down to 1024 x 768. What this means is that you should try to keep your layout width to no more than 950 pixels in order to avoid displaying the horizontal scroll bar. The diagram below shows that fewer than 1% of web users have a resolution lower than 1024 x 768.

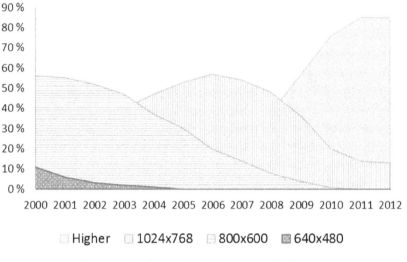

Screen resolution statistics. Source: w3schools.com

Usability Testing

It is hard to be objective about something that you have created. Therefore, it is important to have people other than yourself test your website. This can reveal problems that are not obvious to the designer. Be sure to have the users explore the site fully, and have them give feedback. Ask them to give opinions on, for example, the design, color scheme, content, navigation, organization, forms, and performance of the site.

PART 2

Onsite SEO

CHAPTER 8

Search Engines

Whether you have a content site or an e-commerce site, search engine traffic will constitute a large percentage of your visitors. For a mature site, 25-50% of its traffic will typically come from search engines. Because of this, a continual theme throughout this book is to optimize your website to rank highly in search engines. This concept is called *Search Engine Optimization*, or *SEO* for short. It is the practice of optimizing a site's internal and external aspects to increase the search engine traffic it receives.

Search Engine Comparison

The majority of web traffic is driven by the major search engines—Google, Yahoo, and MSN. Together they account for more than 90% of the US search market, as can be seen below.

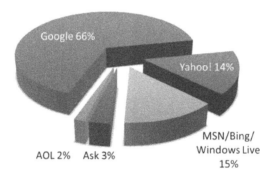

Share of Search. Source: ComScore.com

Why Achieve Top Rankings

In order to generate traffic from search engines it is important to rank near the top of the *Search Engine Result Pages* (SERP). On Google, the first search result receives 36% of the clicks. This is equivalent to getting the traffic resulting from holding the second through fifth positions. In total, the first page receives 89% of the traffic. Therefore, if your site does not appear on the first page, that keyword phrase is unlikely to bring in much traffic. How to track your keyword rankings will be covered in a later chapter.

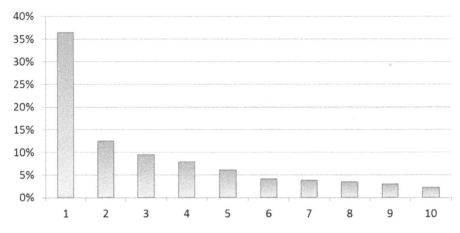

Click-through rate for Google ranking positions. Source: Optify.net

How to Achieve Top Rankings

In this book, SEO techniques for achieving high rankings are divided into two categories: onsite and offsite. In short, the techniques relate to the following.

- **Onsite** – Creating a high quality website, generating content for it and optimizing the site's use of keywords.

- **Offsite** – Acquiring links to the website, particularly from related, high ranking sites.

Usefulness

A search engine makes the best match it can between the words people use when searching and all the web pages it has indexed. These words are called *keywords*. You want people to see your site at the top of the search results for commonly searched keyword phrases that relate to your site. This means more traffic and thus more income.

Since most of your search engine traffic will come from Google, the SEO techniques discussed in this book will implicitly refer to improving your Google rankings. However, such techniques will often improve your rankings in other search engines as well. This is because the goal of search engines is the same—to display the most useful search results they can find to the searchers.

When a user types in a query at Google, the pages returned will be the most useful pages it can find. Usefulness in Google's eyes is a combination of three factors: relevance, reputation, and quality.

- **Relevance** – The pages returned will be relevant to the searched for keywords.

- **Reputation** – The pages shown will be ranked in part according to the quantity and quality of links to these pages.

- **Quality** – The ranking of the pages shown is influenced by the quality of those pages.

Relevance

For a page to appear in the search results for a given keyword phrase, it needs to have content which is relevant to that phrase. The factors Google uses to decide how relevant a page is number in the hundreds. Some of the more important factors used when evaluating a page's relevance to a phrase include:

- **Existence** – Does the exact keyword phrase exist on the page?

- **Proximity** – If the individual keywords are present on the page, how close together are they?

- **Relationship** – Do other related words exist on the page?

- **Positioning** – Where are the keywords located in the text?

- **Subject** – Are the keywords related to the main subject of the page?

- **Co-occurrence** – How frequently do the keywords occur across the page?

Other sites linking to yours will also influence the keywords your pages will be considered relevant for.

- **Anchor text** – Do the keywords exist in the anchor text that links to the page?

- **Context relevance** – Do the keywords appear near the link on the linking page?

As you can see, there are many ways of getting relevance for a keyword phrase, but this is of little use unless the page has reputation as well.

Reputation

When faced with multiple pages of apparently relevant information, Google has to decide which are the most authoritative or trustworthy. This is done by comparing the quality and quantity of the references these pages have in the form of links. Thus, reputation is developed by acquiring links from sites that already have high reputation and that are relevant to yours. The factors that make a link contribute the most to your reputation will be covered later in the chapter on Quality links.

Quality Factors

In addition to relevance and reputation, the quality of your site will also influence Google's decision when ranking your pages. Some of the more important quality factors include those listed below.

- **Responsiveness** – Does the page load quickly?

- **Validation** – Does the page contain errors or poorly written code?

- **Outgoing links** – Does the page link to other relevant, authoritative pages?

- **Site relevance** – Is the page relevant to the rest of the site?

- **Page age** – How long has the page been around? Older pages have more authority.

- **Update frequency** – How often is the page reviewed? Search engines like content that is up to date.

- **Language** – How natural is the language? Does it appear computer generated or spam-like?

These quality factors and many others will be considered as you build (or improve) your site in the coming chapters.

CHAPTER 9

Site SEO

Web Crawlers

Search engines use automated software—known as *web crawlers, robots,* or *spiders*—to search the web and index pages which are then analyzed and ranked. For web crawlers to be able to read your content, it needs to be visible to them. Crawlers basically cannot see anything that is not a piece of text. Content embedded in formats such as Flash, JavaScript and images cannot be read, and therefore it is text lost for boosting your search rankings. This chapter contains some basic rules that will let you avoid this by enhancing your site's visibility to web crawlers.

JavaScript

JavaScript is a client-side scripting language used for creating dynamic web pages. When correctly applied, it can enhance a website and help you achieve many effects that HTML cannot. However, it is important to note that links in JavaScript are not visible to crawlers, and therefore will not be followed. If you have JavaScript menus that you cannot do without, you should make sure there are alternative HTML links towards those destinations, so that all your links will be crawlable.

Flash

Flash is a popular method for adding animation and interactivity to web pages. When used in small amounts, it can enhance a website without damaging its search engine rankings. However, crawlers cannot index the content inside a Flash file or follow Flash links. Therefore, links and content should reside outside Flash's influence.

As a general rule, keep Flash at a minimum. If you feel strongly about using an all Flash page, be sure to create an HTML version of that page as well and block the Flash version of your pages from the crawlers with a robots meta tag.[*] Use Flash where it counts and avoid it whenever there is a reasonable alternative using HTML, CSS or JavaScript.

---

[*]`http://googlewebmastercentral.blogspot.com/2007/03/using-robots-meta-tag.html`

Multimedia

Audio and video are both elements that can enhance a website when used appropriately. For ranking purposes, however, make sure to also create a text-only version of your multimedia whenever possible. As for graphical text, it should be avoided in most situations. Use CSS to style your text so that it will count towards increasing your search rankings.

Other Crawler Blocks

Web crawlers may not index a web page or its links completely if it has one of the characteristics listed below. However, they can make an exception if the page has a significant amount of reputation.

- **Parameters** – Pages with more than two dynamic parameters may not be indexed – for example, "page.php?post=102&cat=5&action=view".

- **Link quantity** – Crawlers may not follow all links from a page containing more than 100 of them.

- **Deep links** – Internal pages more than three links away from the front page may not be followed.

Some pages may be completely inaccessible for web crawlers, particularly if they have one of the attributes below.

- **Login** – Pages requiring a login or cookie to access.

- **Form** – Pages accessible only through an HTML form.

- **Robots** – Pages blocked with the robots meta tag.

▦ **Note** IndexSpy-WP* – This WP plug-in provides a list showing which of your pages Google has indexed.

Canonical URL

Each page should have only one possible URL. Otherwise you may hurt those pages' ranking, because the value that comes from links will be split to multiple versions. This can occur because the CMS you use has several URL paths that all point to the same page, which are accessed through separate forms of navigation on your site. WordPress, with its permalink structure, does not suffer from this problem much.

---

*http://wordpress.org/plugins/indexspy/

Most often, the problem of multiple versions can be found on a site's front page. For example, the following URLs all point to the same page, but are different to search engines:

- `http://yoursite.com`

- `http://www.yoursite.com`

- `http://yoursite.com/index.php`

- `http://www.yoursite.com/index.php`

In WordPress, the index.php version is automatically redirected to the root URL. Likewise, the www and non-www versions are also redirected to the version specified under WordPress address on the Settings ➤ General administration page. The following SEO plug-in will also take care of some other common duplication issues.

Note   All in one SEO pack[*] – This WP plug-in avoids typical duplicate content issues and allows the creation of canonical URLs.

Note that pointing to the front page with or without a "/" at the end does not matter to search engines. Similarly, leaving out the "http://" protocol will not cause the page to be registered as a separate version. The following URLs thus refer to the same version of the front page.

- `http://www.yoursite.com`

- `http://www.yoursite.com/`

- `www.yoursite.com`

- `www.yoursite.com/`

A solution to the issue of multiple page versions is to take any duplicate pages and use a 301 permanent redirect rule[†] to point all versions to a single "canonical" version of the web page. This is done by redirecting the request for a particular URL to another page by adding a couple of code lines to an .htaccess file. You can simplify the task using the plug-in below.

Note   Quick Page/Post Redirect[‡] – This WP plug-in lets you redirect pages and posts to a canonical URL.

---

[*]`http://wordpress.org/plugins/all-in-one-seo-pack/`
[†]`http://www.seomoz.org/articles/301-redirects.php`
[‡]`http://wordpress.org/plugins/quick-pagepost-redirect-plugin/`

Duplicate Content

Google removes pages with duplicate content from its search results. What this means is that if there are multiple pages on the web with virtually the same content, only one of them will be displayed on the search result pages—the one with the highest reputation. Therefore, you should make sure that your content only appears once on your site, and not on any other sites. A tool you can use to discover online plagiarism is Copyscape.[*] If you do republish some of your own content, or with permission someone else's content, it is a good idea to rewrite it a bit first.

Duplicate content is defined rather vaguely by Google as a substantial block of text that is a complete match or appreciably similar. Smaller chunks, snippets, and translated content are not considered duplicates.

---

[*]http://www.copyscape.com

CHAPTER 10

Keyword Research

In order for your website to attract search traffic, you need to create content pages that are optimized for the keywords that people search for within your niche. To discover these keywords, you need to perform a keyword research. If your site will have a limited set of content pages, you can do this research once for all of your pages. Otherwise, if you intend to make a regularly updated site you can do the research for each individual content page just before creating it.

The first step is to head over to Google AdWords Keyword Planner and enter the subject for the content page you are going to create. The tool will show you the global monthly searches for the searched term, as well as for other similar terms. The results displayed can be shown in three ways: broad, [exact], and "phrase" match.

- **Broad match** – Similar phrases and relevant variations. Displayed without quotation marks or square brackets – e.g. golf.

- **Phrase match** – Searches that matches the exact phrase. Displayed inside quotation marks – e.g. "golf".

- **Exact match** – Searches that match the exact phrase exclusively. Displayed inside square brackets – e.g. [golf].

The most relevant results in terms of search volume are the exact matches, so go ahead and filter the search result by selecting the exact match type. Keep in mind that this match may still not be displayed for the searched term if it is not a commonly searched phrase.

☐ Keyword	Competition	Global Monthly Searches	Local Monthly Searches	Local Search Trends
☐ ☆ [golf swing] 🔍 ▨▨▨		40,500	14,800	▬▬▬▬▄▆█▅██
☐ ☆ [golf swing tips] 🔍 ▨▨▨		12,100	5,400	▁▁▁▁▁▄███▆▆
☐ ☆ [golf swing instruction] 🔍 ▨▨▨		1,900	1,000	█▆▄▁▁▄▆▄▄█▅
☐ ☆ [improve golf swing] 🔍 ▨▨		2,400	1,600	▄█▁▄▆▄▁▅▅██
☐ ☆ [perfect golf swing] 🔍 ▨▨▨		6,600	3,600	▁▁▁▁▄▆███▅▆
☐ ☆ [improve your golf swing] 🔍 ▨▨		1,600	880	▄█▄▄██▄▅█▄█
☐ ☆ [golf swing aids] 🔍 ▨▨▨		1,900	1,000	▆█▄▆▄▄█▆███
☐ ☆ [golf swing trainer] 🔍 ▨▨▨		2,900	1,900	█▆▄█████▄█▆
☐ ☆ [golf swing lessons] 🔍 ▨▨▨		1,000	720	▆██▄█████▄▄

An example of a search for the exact term "golf swing" using the Google AdWords Keyword Planner

Go through the results and compile a list of the potential terms you can use as the primary keyword phrase for the content page. For each keyword on your list, write down the global monthly searches. To get more ideas you can vary your searches and also make use of the phrase and broad matching options. Different word order and plurals will typically produce different results, while capitalization will not. You can ignore keywords for which there is not a strong demand—less than 1000 monthly searches. There is no use in creating content that will not be read.

Keyword phrase	Monthly searches
Golf swing	40 500
Golf swing tips	12 100
Golf swing instructions	1 900

Most of the keywords in your list should be 3 to 5 words long. People using longer keyword phrases know what they are looking for and will therefore convert at a significantly higher rate. These terms are also much less competitive than keywords that are 1 to 2 words long. It is possible even for a new site to attain high rankings for a long keyword phrase through limited marketing efforts and page optimizations.

SEO Competition

You now have a list of keyword phrases with a high number of monthly searches. The next step is to determine the competition you would need to beat to take the number one spot for these keywords on Google. Start by searching through the list on Google, one keyword phrase at a time. Click on the top result and analyze that page. You need to determine how solid its hold on the number one position is for that specific keyword phrase. To estimate this you can use a point system by following the checklist below.

Description	Points
PageRank	+PR
Keywords in title	+3
Keywords in domain name	+2
Keywords in heading	+2
Keywords in page name	+1
Keywords in content	+1

The first point in the list is the Google PageRank, which will be explained in a later chapter. The other items refer to where the keywords appear on the page. So if the exact keyword phrase is in the title of the page, you add 3 points. If the keywords are in the wrong order, or if one of them are missing, then add half the points. After you have summed up the final score, add it to your list. Then continue with the next keyword until you have analyzed the competition for all of them.

Keyword phrase	Monthly searches	Competition
Golf swing	40 500	9
Golf swing tips	12 100	5
Golf swing instructions	1 900	6.5

If the competition for a keyword is above 8, remove that keyword. While this book will give you the tools to beat just about any competition, it is much easier to find a less competitive page to go after. For the amount of work required to beat an optimized page, you can get several content pages to the number one spot for less competitive keywords.

You now have enough information to determine which keyword you want to optimize your page for. Pick the keyword that has the highest monthly traffic, combined with a low SEO competition. This will be the page's primary keyword phrase.

Secondary Keywords

Once the primary keyword phrase for the content page has been decided, you want to use the same method for finding secondary keyword phrases. These are the keywords that will appear in the subheadings on the page. They should also show up in the first paragraph, or at least in the content, belonging to each subheading. Secondary phrases will not carry as much weight as the primary one will. Therefore, to rank for these phrases you want to find keywords with really low competition. Such phrases may not bring in a lot of search traffic, but it will be better than nothing.

CHAPTER 11

Using Keywords

In the last chapter, you organized a set of keyword phrases that will become the structure for a new content page. Now it is time to put these keywords to use. Go ahead and create the content page you outlined with only the page name filled in. This is a simple task using your CMS. Do not publish it for others to see. Only create it without any content so that you have something to work with.

By following the guidelines in this chapter you can begin to optimize the content page. These optimizations will help the page rank highly for your keyword phrases later on, once your content has been added and the page is published. Before you go ahead with these guidelines it is recommended that you install the following SEO plug-in if you use a WP site.

Note   All in one SEO pack[*] – This WP plug-in automatically optimizes your site for search engines and allows you to set titles and meta descriptions manually.

Title Tag

Keywords in the <title> element have the highest ranking value with most search engines. The title should therefore contain your most important keywords for each page—the primary keyword phrase. To avoid having the title cut off by some search engines its length should be at most 66 characters, although its importance may warrant additional characters.

The text in your title element shows up in the browser's title bar, on the browser's tab and on bookmarks. It is therefore an important navigation aid for the visitor. The element also shows up in the search result pages as a link back to your page. Thus, it is your most important tool for grabbing the readers' attention, and convincing them to click through on the search engine results page. The title element should therefore be a human-readable summary that accurately describes the overall content of each page, while at the same time targeting your primary keyword phrase for that page.

---

[*]http://wordpress.org/plugins/all-in-one-seo-pack/

One of the metrics Google uses to determine search ranking is known as click popularity. What this means is that if your site is clicked more often than expected on Google's search result pages, this will increase your search ranking for the searched keyword phrase. This is another reason why picking a good title is so important.

Title Guidelines

Below are some guidelines that you should abide by when writing a title.

- **Uniqueness** – The title should be different on every page of your website.

- **Positioning** – Your most important keywords should appear at the beginning of the title.

- **Separators** – Use separators, such as "-", to break the title into sections. Do not repeat keywords back to back.

- **Casing** – Capitalize the first letter of keywords to make them stand out more.

Title Structure

Your front page title should have your site or company name followed by a keyword rich description of your site. Individual pages should include their primary keyword search phrase. Additional keywords you may want to include are:

- **Category** – The category can serve as both a navigational aid and an additional related keyword.

- **Location** – If you are serving only a regional market then including the location in the title is very important.

- **Site name** – Your site name, which preferably includes keywords.

- **Site description** – If there is space left over in your title, you may want to include a keyword rich description of your site.

- **Company name** – If you want to build brand awareness you can include your company name at the end of the titles. Alternatively, use your site name if that is your brand.

Here is an example of how a title for this chapter could look:

```
<title>How to Use Keywords - A Quick Guide to Building an Online
Business - Pro-WebMarketing.com</title>
```

This title will bring in search traffic for the page's primary keyword phrase, the site description and the site name. The first two title sections are 66 characters long, so the last section will be trimmed off on Google.

Meta Tags

Meta tags are HTML elements located in the head section of a document. These tags are not directly visible to visitors. Instead, they are read only by search engine web crawlers and give them information about the document. In addition to the mandatory charset meta tag,[*] your pages can also include the description and keywords meta tags.

Meta Description

The meta description tag can contain a brief keyword rich description of what can be found on the page. Many search engines—such as Google—will show the meta description in the search results below your title if the user's search term exists in the description. This tag therefore gives you some control over what visitors see in the search result pages, though not as much as with the title element.

    The description should give a short marketing message relating to the page, enticing the searcher to click your link rather than the one above or below. To avoid having the description truncated by some search engines, you should use a maximum of 150 characters for this description. The tag is not given any weight in the ranking algorithms of Google so no keyword optimization is necessary. To avoid spending too much time on these tags, you can build the meta description using content from the first one or two paragraphs on the page later when you have created the content.

```
<meta name="description" content="My page description" />
```

Meta Keywords

The meta keywords tag can contain a comma-separated list of the keywords and keyword phrases relevant to the content on the page. This tag is ignored by the major search engines—such as Google, Yahoo, and MSN. Therefore, I recommend leaving this tag out.

```
<meta name="keywords" content="kw one, kw two" />
```

Heading Tags

Keywords in heading elements carry a lot of weight in search engines, with <H1> being the most important and <H6> the least. From the visitors perspective they are also important for visually grouping sections, making the page easier to read and scan. Therefore, be sure to include at least <H1> and <H2> elements on your text content pages.

    Each page is expected to have only one <H1> element. The <H1> element should consist of the page's primary keyword phrase, which is also included in the page title. This will tell the search engine visitor that they have found what they were looking for. It will also tell web crawlers that there is a relation between the title of your page and its headline.

---

[*]http://www.pvtuts.com/html/html-standards#meta-tag

Subheadings (<H2> and <H3>) can hold secondary keyword phrases for the page. Additionally, these headings can contain in-page links to their specific sections of the page. This will add link value to the headings and allow visitors to make direct links to those sections of the page.

```
<h2 id="heading"><a href="#heading">Heading</a></h2>
```

Anchor Links

Internal linking improves your search engine reputation, just as links from outside your site does. An important difference is that you have full control over your internal links—including what the link text is and where they point to.

When providing an internal link using the anchor element, make sure that the anchor text includes concise keywords relating to the target page. This makes the hyperlink more descriptive to your users and to the search engines, which will give the page a greater relevance for the specified keywords.

You can insert the title attribute within the HTML of a text link to add other relevant keywords, and thereby give the target page relevance for them as well. The text within the title attribute will appear when visitors hover over the link with their cursor, so you should make the description useful for your visitors as well as for the search engines.

```
<a title="More Keywords" href="url">Keywords</a>
```

URL

Having keywords in the URLs will give your web pages a small ranking boost. For starters, the page name that appears at the end of the URL should include descriptive keywords without being too long. This way, visitors will also get an additional hint of what to expect on the landing page. Often, the page name can be a shorter version of the <H1> heading that uses dashes (-) as word separators and is lowercase only. You want to include only the keywords and remove the common words—such as "a", "the", and "you". This will keep the page name short and search engine friendly. There is a WP plug-in available that will perform this task automatically.

■ **Note** SEO Slugs[*] – This WP plug-in removes generic words from the page name in order to improve SEO.

---

[*]http://wordpress.org/plugins/seo-slugs/

In addition to the page name, categories can be used in the URL to show where a page belongs in your site's structure. Make sure the category names include keywords, just as the page names do. Well-structured URLs have the additional benefit of serving as their own anchor text when people copy and paste them as links. This gives reputation to the page for the keywords used in the URL. An example of a keyword rich URL is shown below.

```
http://www.programmingvideotutorials.com/php/php-introduction
```

A URL should include as few dynamic parameters as possible. Dynamic parameters are used to pass variables to dynamically generated pages. For example, "post.php?post=103&action=edit" is a dynamic URL that sends two variables to a PHP script called "post.php". Static URLs, which do not include any parameters, are better than dynamic URLs for several reasons:

- Static URLs are typically ranked better in search engine results pages, because they generally contain more keywords.

- Static URLs are indexed faster than dynamic URLs, which may not be indexed at all. Since search engines only want to list pages that are unique they may cut off a dynamic URL after the first two parameters.

- Static URLs make it easier for the user to understand what the page is about, which in turn makes them more likely to click through on the link.

- Static URLs are cleaner and easier to remember for the visitor.

With a WordPress site you can change the URL structure fairly easily. From the Admin Area (located at "your-wordpress-url/wp-admin") select Settings➤Permalinks and choose to specify a custom structure such as, for example, "/%category%/%postname%." If you then group your WordPress posts under appropriate categories, the URL will reflect that structure. Furthermore, once you have configured a custom permalink structure, you will be able to change the permalink page name for a WP post from that post's edit page.

You can find more information about changing permalinks from the WordPress Codex.[*] To avoid losing any page rank you should generate 301 (permanent) redirects from your old dynamic URLs to your new static ones, unless your site is brand new.

Note   Change Permalink Helper[†] – This WP plug-in allows you to change your permalink structure without breaking the old links to your website.

---

[*]http://codex.wordpress.org/Using_Permalinks
[†]http://wordpress.org/plugins/change-permalink-helper/

Images

Images and graphical text can make a site more visually appealing, but it is important to remember that web crawlers cannot look at images or read graphical text. To help crawlers make sense of images, and rate them highly for image search results, there are a couple of things you can do:

- **File Name** – Use a descriptive keyword rich name for the image.

- **Alt** – The alt attribute is designed to provide alternative text when the image cannot be displayed. It should be descriptive of the image.

- **Title** – The title attribute's value shows up in a popup box when the visitor's cursor hovers over the image. It should also describe the image and can therefore often be the same as the alt attribute's value.

- **Proximity** – Keywords close to the image in the same block element should be relevant to the image.

- **Relevancy** – The image should be connected to the page subject to contribute to higher image search rankings.

Note that, even with all of these techniques applied, graphical text is still not as good as ordinary HTML text in terms of SEO.

Keyword Rich Content

Another place where your page's keyword phrases should appear is within the content itself. Do not let too many keywords destroy your content though. You want the keyword phrases to seamlessly flow into the text. They should be virtually undetectable when read by someone with no knowledge of SEO.

Keywords in the first paragraphs of a page weigh more than keywords in the rest of the text. Likewise, words that are bold, italic, and/or underlined are considered more important by search engines. Be sure to only use these styles occasionally, so as not to dilute their value.

CHAPTER 12

Content

Content Types

Text content is only one example of content you may have on your site. The various content types include:

- **Text** – Articles, guides, stories, news, blog posts, and reviews.
- **Audio** – Audio programs, podcasts, and music.
- **Images** – Photos, graphics, info graphs, drawings, and web comics.
- **Videos** – Video seminars, YouTube videos, and video tutorials.
- **Games** – Online games, Flash games, and mobile games.
- **Apps** – Web tools, and other web applications.

Text content has a distinct advantage in terms of increasing your search rankings. Therefore, you should always provide text along with your content, or better still include a plain text version of the content itself if possible.

Authoring High Quality Content

Visitors will not stay long at, return to, buy from or link to a poor quality site. The quality of your site and the value of your content need to be of the highest quality. If they are not, you will always be working upstream against the sites in your niche that are.

Your site does not necessarily have to be the best in its niche, but you should aim for it to be and give an impression of it being. People visiting your site should know that your site may very well be one of the best sites in its niche.

What to Write

From the Keyword Research chapter, you learned how to find out what people want to know within your niche and the keywords they use to express this to Google. In the chapter on Using Keywords, you learned how to use these keywords to optimize your content pages. Now it is time to start creating the content in the content type of your choice.

From a business standpoint, I recommend that you avoid creating content that becomes obsolete quickly and has little residual value, such as news. You want content that will be read more than once. Websites with interesting, focused and original content usually rank well, and so you should aim for that.

Content Generation

If you love writing, then creating your content personally can be both fun and profitable. You should know though, that you do not necessarily have to create the content yourself. Although this method does allow you full control over the content quality, it also requires a significant investment of time. Other ways of generating content include: delegation, collaboration, aggregation, and user submissions.

- **Delegation** – Hire experts in your field to create your content.

- **Collaboration** – Work together with other people or sites to create content more quickly.

- **Aggregation** – Collect and republish existing content. Make sure to first acquire the necessary licenses or permissions from the content owners before you do this.

- **User submissions** – Allow visitors to submit their own content.

CHAPTER 13

Content Pages

First Page Type

Back in the chapter on Site Structure, four different page types were introduced. The first of these were the content pages. These pages offer content in order to increase traffic to your site. No matter what kind of site you run, you need to have something of high value in order to attract and keep visitors. Products and services offered do constitute value, but unless your site is a recognized brand you will have a hard time attracting customers solely by offering goods for sale.

This is where free content comes into play. Your site should provide high quality free content, because it is much easier to market than products and services. Without it, you will have difficulty in increasing your search rankings and traffic.

Free Content

Free content plays a pivotal role in generating traffic, which is the number one key to monetizing a site. A paradox in web business is that you can profit more by giving your content away for free, than you could by charging for it. This is because the traffic you receive with free content is many times higher than that which you get by offering content even at a very low price.

Free content is about generating indirect revenue. The key is to have some other monetization strategy in place to profit from all the traffic generated by the content. Most people will come to your site for the free content, not to buy stuff. However, while they are at your site they will be exposed to your monetization strategies, and a percentage of them will earn you money through them. These strategies will be covered in the fourth part of this book.

If your content is your product, then you should not give all of it away for free. Up to 80% of your content can be free. This will allow you to attract as much traffic as possible, while still retaining enough value for people to purchase that exclusive 20% of your content.

Keyword Specific Content Pages

Content pages on your site should be keyword specific. That is, each page should be focused on a single subject within the site's niche and its related keyword phrases. The more focused your web pages are, the higher they will rank for related search terms. Every bit of content on the page should relate to the subject and anything not related should be left for another page.

The opening paragraph is the most important one, both for search engines and visitors. Use it to describe the content on the rest of the page. Be sure to include your page's primary keyword phrase in this opening paragraph. This will help you get better search engine rankings for that phrase.

Content Update Frequency

One of the most effective methods to keep people returning to your website is to make sure that it has regularly updated content. If this is a strategy you intend to use for your site, then set a schedule to add a new page of quality content, for example daily or at least weekly. This will not only help your site rankings, but your visitors will know when to expect updates and will come often to see what is new. If your site does not require a continuous release of new content, be sure to at least show that the site has been reviewed recently and is up to date.

When you start to acquire a large amount of traffic, producing more high quality content often becomes a better investment of time than marketing your site. Each new content page you add acts as a new entry point into your site that your visitors may share with the world. Still, your focus should be on quality before quantity. Investing a significant amount of time producing a few pages of exceptional quality is easily more valuable and a better use of your time than a hundred average pages targeting every conceivable keyword.

Content Length

The total word count of a content page should be at least 250 words. Otherwise it may get passed over for high rankings. On the other hand, do not make pages so long that they become difficult to overview and lose focus. This is not only bad for SEO, but longer articles can have a high drop off rate in readers. If a web page covering one topic has more than a couple of pages, you should consider splitting it up into sub topics that are covered on separate web pages.

Structure Formatting

Make your content pages easy to scan and visually appealing by properly structuring your content in the following ways.

- **Headings** – Organize your content into sections and subsections by using headings. Make sure the visitor can always see at least one heading on the screen.

- **Paragraphs** – Use the paragraph element to explicitly delimit your content into short blocks that are easily scannable. Short – 3 to 5 line – paragraphs add whitespace and visual relief to text-heavy pages.

- **Lists** – Ordered/unordered lists help break long paragraphs into easily scannable content. The ideal length for a bulleted list is 3 to 5 items. Whole sentences work better than just listing phrases.

- **Tables** – Use table markup for tabulating data into rows and columns. It is not to be used for page layout.

- **Images** – Images are a great way to break up text-heavy pages. They can add whitespace and color to your pages and help with search engine optimization.

- **Emphasis and strong emphasis** – Use these font styles in small quantities to draw attention to important text within your content.

- **Links** – Use links in the content to direct your readers to more information and to internal related pages.

Style Formatting

Here are some additional guidelines in relation to the style of your content pages and their content.

- **Whitespace** – Leave plenty of whitespace. Without it the design will feel crowded and unbalanced.

- **Font** – Use an easy to read font – such as Verdana, Arial or Times – in a standard size.

- **Line height** – A line height of around 150% will improve the readability of your content.

- **Spell check** – Make sure to carefully spell check any content you add to the site. Typographical errors will hurt your site's credibility. Ideally, you should have at least one other person proofread your writing.

- **Sentences** – Use short declarative sentences and simple words for factual text. Do not use long sentences when short ones will work, and do not use long words when short ones will do.

- **Professionalism** – Remove unnecessary definitions, explanations, subjective adjectives and superlatives.

CHAPTER 14

Navigation

Your site's navigation is an important part of providing a pleasant user experience and can aid your SEO efforts. Navigation refers to the way in which a user moves through the content of a website. It is vital that a clear and simple navigation system is used. It should answer these three questions for the visitor:

- Where am I?
- Where have I been?
- Where can I go?

You need to make it as simple as possible for visitors to navigate your site, and access your content and products. Preferably, visitors should be able to find any page within 2 to 3 clicks of any other page. To achieve this, providing them with multiple ways of navigating the site is important.

Just like external links, the site's internal linking structure is a major ranking factor – a factor that is under your complete control. Search engines view pages that require fewer clicks from the front page as having higher importance than pages that require more clicks. They also take into account the anchor text used in the links and how well your pages are interlinked.

Main Navigation

The main navigation system usually takes the form of a menu containing links. This menu should be clearly visible above the fold and remain consistent with the same format in the same place on every page—either to the top left, top center or top right.

Your main menu should contain a link to your front page as well as any main categories. Each link within your navigational structure needs a descriptive anchor text indicating where it will take the user. The anchor text should also correlate with a keyword that you are trying to rank the page for. Use short, preferably one-word links in the menu. Avoid Flash, JavaScript or other crawler hostile links. Instead, use CSS to style the menu.

Footer Navigation

Links to general pages of minor importance can be placed at the bottom of the page—your privacy policy and sitemap pages, for example.

Search Navigation

If your site is large you should include a search mechanism to help visitors find what they are looking for faster. Place the search box in a prominent place so that it is easy to find from any page.

▪ **Note**   Google Custom Search[*] – This WP plug-in allows you to easily integrate a Google Custom Search[†] on your website.

Sequential Navigation

If you have a group of pages that can be sequenced you should provide links from one page to the next/previous ones, so that the visitor can navigate through them more easily.[‡]

Sequential pages may also benefit from keyboard navigation. The left and right arrow keys, for example, can be used to navigate back and forth within the sequence. This can be achieved using JavaScript.

Breadcrumb Navigation

Breadcrumbs—such as Home ➤ Products ➤ Books—allow visitors to see their location relative to the front page. They also provide links back to each parent page in the site hierarchy. This gives you an additional place to include keyword rich links pointing to each page of your site. Breadcrumbs typically appear horizontally across the top of the web page.

Contextual Navigation

Be sure to include internal links from within your content to other related content or reference content on your site. This is a simple and clever way to increase the reputation of other pages within your site with targeted keyword phrases.

▪ **Note**   SEO Smart Links[§] – This WP plug-in automatically links keywords to any relevant pages on your site.

---

[*]http://wordpress.org/plugins/google-custom-search
[†]http://www.google.com/cse/
[‡]http://codex.wordpress.org/Next_and_Previous_Links
[§]http://wordpress.org/plugins/seo-automatic-links/

CHAPTER 15

Navigation Pages

Second Page Type

The second page type a site can have is the *navigation page*. In addition to the navigation elements present on all of your pages, your site may include these dedicated navigation pages. They are pages containing mainly links to content and sales pages to aid the visitor in finding what they are looking for.

Make sure to keep your navigation pages uncluttered and easy to overview. Do not just display a list of links on them—include descriptions as well. If the page lists products, make sure to display images of those products.

Front Page

Your most important navigation page is the front page. This page should make it obvious to the visitor what your site has to offer. It commonly includes summaries and links to the latest and most popular content/products on your site, so that visitors can quickly find what they are looking for.

Search Result Page

Display the search results in a list similar to Google's—that is, a list sorted by relevance made up of the page title followed by the part of the content where the searched term occurs. Be sure to highlight the terms matching the user's search query. This of course is what Google Custom Search will give you, as was mentioned in the last chapter.

Category Pages

A site with many content or sales pages will benefit from grouping these pages according to categories or even sub-categories. When the user navigates to a certain category they are shown a summary of the pages belonging to that category. These can include content pages and sales pages, as well as other navigation pages.

Tag Pages

Many CMS sites provide a fast way to generate navigation pages through the use of tags.[*] Tags are a list of labels you associate with a page. They are similar to categories, but they are not organized into any hierarchy. A page may be listed in multiple tag groups.

When editing a page in your CMS, you can add a number of tags that describe the content of that page. These tags are commonly displayed when viewing the page, usually as a list near the bottom. When the visitor clicks on one of the tags, it brings up a navigation page listing all pages that are tagged with that label.

■ **Note** Simple Tags[†] – This WP plug-in adds advanced tag management capabilities to your site – including tag suggestion, mass edit of tags and auto linking of tags in content.

Sitemap

Providing a sitemap can help search engines and users traverse your site. Every page on your site should be linked to from the sitemap, and every page should link to the sitemap. This will allow visitors and search engine crawlers to find any page in just two clicks. If your site is more than 100 pages, a better choice is to have the sitemap link only to the category pages instead.

There are two types of sitemaps: XML and HTML sitemaps. An XML sitemap lists URLs with optional metadata—such as last modified date, priority, and change frequency. You can submit these to search engines if you are having trouble getting your pages indexed, but improving your site navigation and reputation should solve this.

■ **Note** Google XML Sitemaps[‡] – This WP plug-in will automatically generate an XML sitemap for you. Additionally, it notifies all major search engines every time you add new content.

An HTML sitemap provides an additional way for visitors to navigate your site, and gives you another source of quality links with potential descriptive text for your internal pages.

■ **Note** HTML Page Sitemap[§] – This WP plug-in allows you to add a customizable HTML sitemap to your site.

---

[*]http://en.support.wordpress.com/posts/categories-vs-tags/
[†]http://wordpress.org/plugins/simple-tags/
[‡]http://wordpress.org/plugins/google-sitemap-generator/
[§]http://wordpress.org/plugins/html-sitemap/

PART 3

Marketing

CHAPTER 16

Increasing Traffic

Offsite Promotion

If you have built a good site and are expecting people to just show up, you will be waiting a very long time. While developing a great website is half the work, the other half is promotion. The reality of the Internet is that no matter how great your site is, you still have to promote it. You may receive some small amount of search engine traffic through optimizing your site alone, but to really lift your site off the ground, promoting it is a necessity. Online site promotion comes in two major forms: link building and PPC.

- **Link building** – Acquiring links to your site, particularly quality links that come from related, high ranking sites. This raises your natural search rankings and brings in traffic directly.

- **PPC** – Buying visitors. This can be a viable option if your site has a strong monetization system in place and a high conversion rate.

Where does Traffic come from

There are three ways visitors can arrive at your website: through search engines, referring links and direct traffic.

1. **Search engines** – The user finds your site through a search engine.

2. **Referring links** – The user follows a link from a site or another source.

3. **Direct traffic** – The user arrives through a bookmark or types the URL in manually.

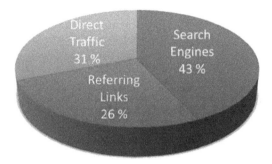

Example of traffic type distribution

In most cases, direct traffic represents returning visitors. These will hopefully make up a good deal of your traffic, since this signifies that your site has a lot of value. On the other hand, search engine traffic and referring link traffic are just as important, because this is how most new users find their way to your site.

Google Analytics

To track and analyze your own site's statistics you should set up your site with Google Analytics.[*] This is a free online service that generates detailed statistics about your site's visitors and their behavior. By tracking this data you will be able to make adjustments to improve your site in many ways.

After adding your site to your profile at Google Analytics, you need to include a tracking script in your site template. You can add the necessary JavaScript code manually or, if you prefer, install a plug-in that does it for you.

■ **Note**   Google Analytics for WordPress[†] – This plug-in integrates Google Analytics with your WordPress site.

Once set up, the service will begin gathering information about your visitors. After a couple of days you should begin to see some results. Be sure to have a look through the many pages of Google Analytics to see what metrics you have at your disposal. Most of your site's important statistics are available on the Overview pages for the various categories.

---

[*]http://www.google.com/analytics/
[†]http://wordpress.org/plugins/google-analytics-for-wordpress/

- **Audience ➤ Overview** – Shows you the number of daily visitors in a graph. A key metric for the popularity of your site and the success of your marketing efforts. Also shows graphs for unique visitors, page views, pages per visit, and many other interesting metrics.

- **Traffic Sources ➤ Overview** – Displays your site's distribution of search, referral, and direct traffic. It can show you exactly which search keywords and referral pages are sending your site its traffic.

- **Content ➤ Overview** – Includes which pages get the most traffic. You may want to produce more content similar to these pages, or turn such pages into a series. Other pages can also be changed to emulate these high traffic pages to improve their popularity.

Google Webmaster Tools

Another Google site you want to start using is Google Webmaster Tools[*] (GWT). This site contains a collection of tools that give you useful information about your site from Google's point of view. Most importantly, it shows you the search ranking positions you hold and some of the back links that Google knows of. Go there now to register and verify your site, if you have not done so already. This SEO information will be important as you begin building links to your site. Once you have verified yourself as the owner of your site, you can use GWT to tell you about a number of things related to your site. Some of the more important pages include:

- **Search queries** – This page shows which keyword phrases you rank for and the exact ranking position you currently hold.

- **Links to your site** – Shows which sites link to you and with how many back links. Also shows which of your pages have the most back links.

- **Internal links** – Here you can see how well your pages are interlinked.

- **Crawl errors** – Lists any problems encountered by Google's crawlers while on your site, such as unfound pages and broken links. Be sure to fix any broken links, and if there are unfound pages you may want to redirect these to their intended locations.

- **HTML improvements** – Displays any potential problems with your pages.

---

[*]http://www.google.com/webmasters/

CHAPTER 17

Link Building

Links are the currency of sites.

About Back Links

Back links, also known as external or inbound links, are links from other websites directed towards your site. Such links give two benefits. They bring traffic directly from people clicking the links, and also indirectly from boosting your search engine rankings.

In terms of ranking, every link to your site is seen by search engines as a vote for your website, improving your rankings accordingly. As for traffic, each back link adds another entryway to your site, giving you more referral traffic. Links to your site are the second most important ranking factor after the page title.

Link Building Strategies

Link building can be grouped into two types of strategies: artificial and natural.

- **Artificial link building** – This is where you directly target a site or group of people and try to get back links from them.

- **Natural link building** – These strategies involve indirectly attracting back links through improving the quality of your site and content.

These two strategies will be discussed in later chapters.

Traffic or Ranking

Generally, the traffic that a link can bring you is more valuable than the reputation it conveys. The purpose of increasing your search ranking is to generate more traffic, so getting the traffic directly from the link is a much more effective means of achieving this. The increased traffic from the link also means that you have additional traffic that provides natural linking, assisting you in your link building efforts.

Discover Existing Back Links and Rankings

Before you start a link building campaign, you need an easy way to keep track of your rankings and incoming links to determine how well your campaign performs. As mentioned in the last chapter, your Google search rankings are readily available at Google Webmasters Tools. The Search queries page provides an accurate listing of which keyword phrases you currently rank highly for, and which ones you may want to market some more.

Additionally, Google Webmasters Tools lists back links to your site under the "Links to your site" page. There you can also find the anchor text used in the back links, which should hopefully include keywords related to your site. Be aware that Google will not show you all the back links that it knows about and uses to determine your rankings. It will only show a seemingly random sample of links, probably to make it more difficult for webmasters to determine the full effectiveness of their link building campaigns. For more accurate lists of back links, you can use Bing's Site Explorer* or Seomoz's Open Site Explorer.†

Be sure to download a copy of the back links you find, and a copy of the search ranking table, before starting your marketing campaign. This will allow you to accurately measure the success of your marketing efforts.

Measuring your Site Rank

There are a number of ways to measure your site rank, the most accurate of which is Alexa.‡ Alexa ranks sites based on their estimated traffic levels. This information is in large part provided by users of its Alexa Toolbar and other browser plug-ins using their data. To see your site's rank, just run a search on their site for your domain name and it will display a wide range of valuable metrics for free—including traffic rank, trends, regional data, inbound links, average load time, top keywords, demographics analyses, page views per user, bounce rate and time on site. Note that for Alexa to provide any reliable statistics your site will have to be fairly popular, ranking at least in the top 1 million.

Since the Alexa rank measures traffic levels, it can be used to give a rough estimate of how much traffic a site receives. The following graph illustrates this by showing how a site's Alexa rank can correspond to the number of average unique daily visitors.

---

*http://www.bing.com/toolbox/webmaster
†http://www.opensiteexplorer.org/
‡http://www.alexa.com

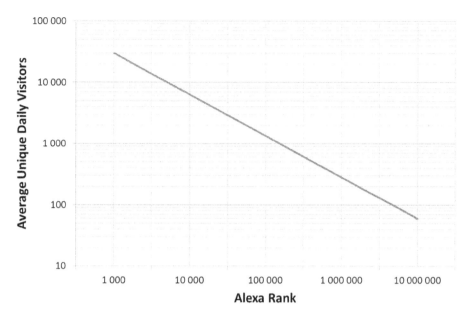

Traffic levels and Alexa rank. Source: `Webs9.com`

Another common way of measuring site rank is through Google's PageRank (PR) metric. PageRank assigns a number between 0 and 10 to web pages based on their importance in the eyes of Google. In essence, the PageRank for a page is determined by considering the number of pages that link to that one page, and the individual PageRank for those linking pages. The more pages that link in, and the greater PageRank they have, the greater PageRank the linked to page will get.

The exact method for calculating PageRank has not been disclosed by Google. Furthermore, the displayed PageRank value is not the actual value Google uses to rank search results, and it is only updated every three months or so, making it a very rough metric. Nonetheless, pages with a high PageRank are more likely to appear at the top of search results for relevant search terms.

If you use Firefox, you can view both the Alexa rank and PageRank, conveniently displayed on the status bar, by installing the Search Status Firefox plug-in. This is a very powerful plug-in for web marketers that you should familiarize yourself with fully. One of its many useful features is the ability to highlight nofollow links.

░ **Note** Search Status* – This Firefox plug-in allows you to see the rankings of any website you visit.

---

*http://www.quirk.biz/searchstatus/

Nofollow

A nofollow link, as opposed to a dofollow link, is a link that contains the rel = "nofollow" attribute. Such a link will not increase your search engine reputation. The attribute is designed specifically for search engines, in order to reduce the effectiveness of comment spam. It is currently supported by all major search engines—including Google, Yahoo, and MSN.

```
<a href="url" rel="nofollow">Nofollow link</a>
```

Most blogging software—such as WordPress—automatically assigns the nofollow attribute to links in user submitted comments. Many other popular sites—for example Wikipedia, Digg, del.icio.us, and Yahoo Answers—also use nofollow on their pages. Although nofollow links will not affect your rankings, the traffic and visibility they bring your site can often make it worth your while to go after them in the same way as dofollow links.

Note that the nofollow attribute cannot be used to control the flow of PageRank within your own website. Any link with the nofollow attribute decreases the PageRank that a page can pass on, just as a dofollow link does.

Outgoing Links

Who you link to can have a strong impact on your search rankings. If you link to other trustworthy sites of authority, then you are essentially associating yourself with those sites. It shows that you know where the valuable content in your field is, and that you want to share that content with your visitors. Outgoing links can also work against you. If you link to low quality, junk sites that will serve to decrease your site's value. Therefore, make sure that you mainly link out to high quality, relevant sites that you think your visitors will find useful. Do not link to sites that you would not want to visit yourself.

Outgoing links provide another benefit in that they can automatically generate inbound links in the form of trackbacks. When you publish content that links to another site, a truncated summary of your content will appear on the linked to page, provided that both sites are trackback-enabled. This is the default behavior for most blogging software, including WordPress. However, site owners may decide to disable this feature in order to prevent spamming.

■ **Note** BM-TrackPing* – This WP plug-in automatically groups trackbacks and separate them from the comment list.

```
*http://wordpress.org/plugins/bm-comments-and-trackbacks/
```

Junk Sites

Search engines recognize that you cannot stop people from linking to you. Therefore, links from low quality, junk sites or link farms will usually not hurt you. At worst, the link will not pass any link value to your site or any other sites. However, if you are reciprocating with a link back to them, then it most certainly will.

Buying Search Rankings

Links purchased purely for SEO benefits are not looked on favorably by search engines. Google will penalize sites they find doing that, by devaluing their back links. If link buying is a strategy you intend to use you should focus on buying links from highly ranked sites that are relevant to yours. Avoid buying site wide links, as search engines will not give your site much reputation for them. Instead, focus mainly on in-content links and front page links.

CHAPTER 18

Quality Links

Quality back links are one of the most important factors in building your search engine reputation. It is not enough just to have a lot of back links. It is the quality of back links more than the quantity that will help you rank better in search engines.

Quality links do not just appear randomly—you have to work for them. Acquiring these links may be time-consuming, but they will benefit your site greatly for as long as they remain. While you may not have complete control over who links to you naturally, quality links are what you should aim for in your artificial link building efforts.

There are four main categories that search engines look at when evaluating a link's quality: site attributes, page attributes, relevance, and anchor text. Each one will be looked at in turn.

Site Attributes

The first quality factors relate to the website linking to your site. A link has a higher quality if it has the following attributes.

- **Rank** - They come from sites with a high number of quality back links. The more highly ranked the site is the more it will impact your search ranking.

- **Popularity** - The site the link resides on has a lot of traffic. The more traffic the site has the more visitors it can refer to your site.

Page Attributes

The next quality factors are those relating to the page linking in to your site.

- Link quantity - The value of a link on a page increases the fewer links the page contains. Additionally, an external link appearing site-wide on every page may even be completely devalued.

- Link age - Long held links weigh more heavily than new links. The value of a link therefore increases over time.

- Permanence - You should aim for permanent links. The ranking boost a link provides is lost when it is no longer there.

Link Relevance

Concentrate your link building efforts around sites within niches similar to your own. These are not only much more valuable in terms of search ranking, but visitors to those sites will also be more interested in your site, and therefore be more likely to click through to it. There are three types of relevance: niche, page, and context relevance.

- **Niche relevance** – A link from a site related to your site's niche is better than one that is not, in terms of both the ranking value it provides and the traffic it generates.

- **Page relevance** – The subject of the linking page and the linked to page should be related to provide the most ranking and traffic value.

- **Context relevance** – A link from inside an on-topic paragraph carries greater weight than a link from outside the content, for example, in the sidebar or footer.

Anchor Text

Anchor text is one of the most powerful link ranking components. In terms of SEO, the best links are simple HTML text links. The anchor text of the link should include the descriptive keywords that you have optimized the page to rank for. Search engines use this text to help determine the subject matter of the linked to document. To make your links seem more natural, you should mix up the anchor text a bit with different keyword phrases.

CHAPTER 19

Artificial Link Building

The idea behind including back links as part of the page ranking algorithms is that if a page is good people will start linking to it. In reality, however, a new site cannot always rely on the fact that, if its content is good, people will find it and link to it—at least not in the quality and quantity of back links that you may need to reach your traffic and income goals.

This is where artificial link building comes in—going out there and increasing your back links one link at a time. While this may seem like a daunting task, keep in mind that the time investment is up to you. The steps for manually building quality links are simple enough:

- **Desired back link list** – Compile a list of quality sites related to your site's niche from which you want back links.

- **Adding links** – Add a back link on each of these sites either through a comment, message, guest post or by asking the webmaster to include one.

Desired Back Link List

The first step is to compile a list of high ranking, quality sites in your niche—sites that are authoritative and which would be really valuable to add to your link profile. These are websites that should be worth putting in some extra effort for. There are a couple of ways to find these sites.

- Competitor analysis – Check where your competitors have received their most valuable back links from.

- Searching for back links – Search Google to discover quality sites relevant to yours.

- Back link tools – Use an online tool to discover potential back link sites.

Competitor Analysis

Sites that link to your competitors are probably interested in linking to your site as well. To identify your competitors, enter your site's niche into Google Search and review the links of the top sites that appear. Then you can use the TouchGraph Google Browser* to get a good overview of their back links. This is the link neighborhood you want to be in to rank as well as they do. It is also a good way to get natural traffic, as these are the links and sites that send your competitors much of their traffic.

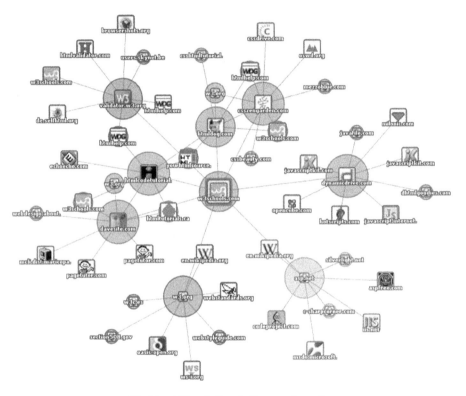

The TouchGraph Google Browser in action

An alternative way to mine the back links of your competitors is to perform a search with Seomoz's Open Site Explorer. Simply type in the URL of a competitor and you will be able to find the inbound links that Seomoz knows about.

You may also want to include the top Google search results on your desired back link list. If a page ranks particularly well for search phrases that you are targeting, a link from that page will be very valuable.

---

*http://www.touchgraph.com/TGGoogleBrowser.html

Searching for Back Links

Another quick way to find related sites where you can place back links is to search for them on Google using the right keyword combination. Below are a number of such keywords to get you started.

- Add/Submit/Suggest/Recommend/Nominate +

- Link/Site/Page/URL/Article/Profile/Resource/Directory +

- Your keywords

Simply type in a combination of these keywords together with one of your site's keywords. For example, if you are trying to market a website selling golf clubs you could search for: "add site" "golf clubs."

Back Link Tools

There are a variety of free tools available that can help you acquire quality back links. One such tool is Webconfs's Backlink Builder Tool.* When you enter the keywords of your choice, the Backlink Builder gives you a list of related sites where you can post a comment, article, message or simply a back link to your site. Some other tools you may want to try out are: Hub Finder† and Link Suggestion Tool.‡

Adding Back Links

At this stage you should have built a large list of sites from which you want to acquire back links. However, different site types will require different strategies for getting these links. The following strategies will be looked at in turn.

- **Profile** – On any site where you can register for an account, you can usually also add a back link in your profile.

- **Posts** – Community sites can be a good place to post messages containing relevant back links.

- **Comments** – Blog sites often allow visitors to add comments with links.

- **Guest posts** – All content sites need content, which you can provide in exchange for back links.

- **Link exchanges** – On any site you can contact the webmaster and ask to exchange links.

---

*http://www.webconfs.com/backlink-builder.php
†http://training.seobook.com/hubfinder/
‡http://tools.seobook.com/general/link-suggest/

Profile

Sites allowing user registration often give their members access to a profile page that is under their control to some extent. You want to make full use of this page on any and all sites related to your niche that allow a profile. Most importantly, include one or even a couple of back links to your site.

Profile links will often be nofollow. However, they can provide some traffic, particularly on sites where you are an active contributor. On such sites users may click through from one of your contributions to your profile to learn more about you. Take this chance to sell them on the idea of clicking through to your site as well, through a short yet interesting description of your site.

Posts

Participating in community sites can be a great way to acquire quality back links. Discover sites that have an established community in your niche and start contributing. Focus on being more helpful than promotional, but when you find a topic directly related to a page on your site be sure to include a direct link to that page. There are various types of community sites on the web:

- **Forums** - Participate in discussion boards related to your site's niche. Make sure to include a back link in your signature line.

- **Groups** - Online discussion groups, such as Google groups.*

- **Q&A** - Answer questions related to your niche and refer people to your site for additional information - for example, Yahoo Answers,† Answers.com,‡ and Mahalo§ provide such a service.

- **Social bookmarking** - Submit link bait and comment on submitted articles related to your site on, for example, Digg.‖

- **Social media sites** - Comment on user submitted content, such as relevant YouTube videos.

- **Social networking** - Join active groups related to your niche on sites like Facebook.

---

*http://groups.google.com
†http://answers.yahoo.com
‡http://www.answers.com
§http://www.mahalo.com
‖http://www.digg.com

Comments

You can post legitimately useful comments on high traffic blogs that are similarly-themed with your site. Be sure to actually read the article and offer, for example, some additional information or insight on what they have written. You want to make it apparent that you are an expert in the field, but do not openly confront the author, since he might just remove your comment.

Blogs often allow you to include a web address along with your name and reply. Use this to link to your front page. When you have a page of your own closely related to the subject of the blog post, you can also include a direct link to that page. Keep in mind that spamming blogs with irrelevant links will make your site look bad. Although links in blog comments are often nofollow, many people will read the comments. Some will also click through to your site to read more of what you have to say, particularly if you leave a relevant, interesting and useful comment.

Guest Posts

Content sites all have something in common—they need content. If you offer your free services as a guest writer or content producer for high-ranking content sites in your niche, they are likely to accept. You provide them for free with something they need—content—and in return they give you what you want—a quality back link included in your content. It is a fair trade.

Guest posts can also be exchanged with other sites. You create a piece of content for their site—such as an article—and they create one back for you. This way, regular visitors to one site can become aware of the other site in the same niche, and they may decide to become a regular visitor to that site as well.

Link Exchange

In a link exchange, one webmaster places a dofollow link on his website that points to another webmaster's site and vice versa. Such reciprocal links from related sites are ranked lower by search engines than one way links. However, it may still be valuable, in terms of SEO, to pursue such links for sites that are highly relevant to yours. The traffic increase from exposing your site to their visitors can also be worth a lot.

When you contact a webmaster to ask for a link exchange, make sure your email is polite and appears personal. This will greatly enhance your chances of success and prevent the recipient from sending the mail straight to the trash bin. In your email, address the webmaster by his or her name if you can find it. Then clearly explain that you want to exchange links and describe how you believe a link to your site would benefit their visitors, and vice versa. Make your offer sound appealing and also tell them briefly about your website.

In the email, you can add your direct contact information—full name, company name, address, and phone number—to increase your perceived credibility. Make it easy for them to link to you by including the standard link exchange information: the link title, URL, and a short site description. Alternatively, you can link to a page on your site offering a variety of link alternatives—such as banners, buttons, and text links.

Give a suggestion as to where the links will be placed. Typically, you do not want your exchanged links to show up on the front page of the site you are promoting. Although that is where the link will provide the most referral traffic and search ranking, it is a limited space that can easily become cluttered. It is more common either to place the links on a separate link page, or to perform a three-way link exchange. In contrast to the regular two-way exchange, a three-way exchange is where you let another site under your control perform your part of the link exchange. This allows you to link from a site that more closely matches the PageRank and Alexa rank of the site you want to link exchange with, so as to ensure a more equal trade. It can also be used to make the link look more natural to search engines, because your second site can be one that appears to be completely unaffiliated with your main site.

Some webmasters may not want to exchange links with you, particularly if their website far outranks yours. Plan to offer an incentive to such webmasters, in addition to the back link. For example, you could offer to do a review of one of their products on your site, or to create a piece of content for their site. Be generous with your incentive and you will gain more links.

Username and Reputation

While you are link building, you can at the same time work on building a strong professional reputation. Begin by choosing a distinct and memorable username that you will use on all sites within your niche. You may want to consider a name that includes keywords related to your site. This is because your name will often appear next to your website link, giving your link a higher relevance for those terms. Additionally, the name you choose will become the anchor text for your site on some blogging systems.

By entering the same username and using the same voice, each time you make a quality contribution to a site within your niche, you will start to build reputation and recognition. Since the people interested in your niche will often visit the same sites that you are link building on, they may come to see your contributions on multiple sites as well, further boosting your authority. This reputation will work in your favor. People recognizing you as an authority in the field are more likely to click through to your site, trust its content, link to the content and even buy from you.

Natural and Artificial Links

Search engines do not like manipulation of their search results through too much artificial link building, or link spamming. A site found guilty of this can be penalized and have its search rankings reduced, or it may even be banned completely. Getting banned from search engines because of artificial link building is a subject of much debate, however. It happens, but only in extreme cases. For example, a brand new site over-promoting itself using an automated tool to generate 1000's of links from low quality sites with the same anchor text is begging to be banned.

Using manual methods, it is exceedingly rare to be penalized. Still, it can pay off to put some effort into making your links appear as natural as possible, if only to make sure that they are not devalued. So what is the difference between a natural link and an artificial one? Simply speaking, a natural back link is made by others while an artificial link is made by you, in order to boost your search rankings and traffic. However, Google cannot know who posts a link, so it has to look for other attributes. Below is a summary of these attributes and how you can adjust them to make your links appear more natural.

- **Anchor text** – Avoid repetitive anchor text. Very important.

- **Link acquisition rate** – Build links at a consistent rate.

- **Link source** – Avoid acquiring links from low quality sites and link farms. Such links are devalued anyway.

- **Deep links** – Acquire links to all your important pages, not just your front page.

- **Different tactics** – Avoid using the same link building tactic repetitively, for example by only getting back links from forum signatures.

The link acquisition rate warrants some additional explanation. Getting 1000 links one month and 10 the next will not appear natural and may raise a red flag for search engines. You should instead try to build a consistent amount of links every couple of days until you reach your traffic goals. Note that web crawlers do not search all sites on the web at all times, so links will not be indexed immediately after you make them. Some may take a day, while others may take several weeks to be indexed, depending on the reputation and update frequency of the site hosting the link. Therefore, you may not have to build a consistent amount of links on a daily basis, but more on a weekly basis.

The average daily number of links you want to acquire for your site during your link building campaign is up to you. Rather than trying to build as many links as possible in this time, you should aim only for quality links. Finding and acquiring these quality links will of course require more time and effort than finding just any link. For example, 5 or 10 quality links per day may be a good place to start. Increase it gradually as you become more proficient at finding these links. Towards the end of your campaign you can gradually decrease your artificial link acquisition rate. By then, you should hopefully have attracted enough traffic so that your visitors contribute back links to your site at a faster rate than you did through your own link building efforts.

CHAPTER 20

Natural Link Building

Attracting back links naturally without working for them may seem like an impossible task for many new website owners, but it is actually quite simple. The more value you provide, the larger a percentage of your visitors will link to your site—through social media and on their own websites. They will link to your site not because they want to support it, but because they believe your site will offer value to their friends or website visitors.

If you have few visitors, naturally the number of monthly back links you attract will be low as well. What you need to resort to then is artificial link building, which was the subject of the previous chapter. However, there comes a point when you have so many visitors that the value you receive from natural back links far exceeds the value from artificial link building. At that stage, you can stop manually building links and instead focus on strategies for increasing the percentage of your visitors that link back to your site naturally, which is the subject of this chapter.

Quality Content

Quality content is the number one key to natural link building. This is because the most important factor in getting people to link to you is to have something worth linking to—high quality content. Provided that you already have a decent amount of traffic, some of the best link building strategies you can employ are those involved in building quality content and improving the site for your visitors. Interesting, link-worthy content will naturally be passed along on social media sites, giving you more and more natural back links.

Link Baiting

The term link bait means to create content that naturally attracts back links by getting people to talk about it through social media. It can be one of the most efficient ways of getting back links, so you should definitely try it out. Although the average quality of the links from a mass link bait campaign is usually relatively low, the amount of links can be very high.

When attempting to create link bait, the keywords to aim for are *interesting* and *relevant*. You want the content to attract a lot of attention, while at the same time being relevant to your site's niche. For examples of link bait content, visit the front page of Digg and other social bookmarking sites. Find out what kind of content related to your niche has made it to the top lists of these sites, and see if you can produce something similar.

There are some topics that are considered more or less universally interesting. For example, content that is funny, useful or controversial tends to fall into this category and makes great link bait.

- **Funny** – Entertainment through high quality videos, pictures or stories can get a lot of people linking.

- **Useful** – Genuinely useful online tools, free products, and automated services can be very link-worthy. Similarly, how-to guides and top-10 lists tend to work well as link bait.

- **Controversial** – Articles about controversial topics dividing your commenting visitors into two sides can work wonders in terms of attracting back links.

Another idea is to tweak content you already have to make it more link-worthy.

Onsite Marketing

There are a number of onsite marketing techniques you can use to encourage visitors to help market your site.

Social Media Links

You should make it easy for social media users to share your pages and to vote for them. This can be done by putting social media links at the bottom of your content and sales pages, which include the URL of the current page ready to be submitted. There are plenty of free social bookmarking plug-ins available.

■ **Note**   Sociable* – This plug-in lets you add social bookmarking and networking buttons to your WordPress site.

Keep the number of social media buttons limited, so that you do not appear too eager for back links. Just stick with the four or so most popular ones—Digg, StumbleUpon, Facebook, and Twitter, for instance.

Examples of social media buttons: Digg, StumbleUpon, Facebook, and Twitter

---

*http://wordpress.org/plugins/sociable/

PDF Printing

By allowing visitors access to a PDF or print friendly version of your text content, they may help market the site for you. For example, they may print the PDF and share it offline or distribute the file online, both of which are often in your best interest. Just make sure to include back links in the PDF or print friendly versions.

Note   Print Friendly* – This WP plug-in cleans your pages for printing and lets visitors download a PDF version of the content.

Link to Us Page

This page includes a set of links that you suggest people can use when linking to your site. On the page you encourage the visitors to share the site with others if they have found it useful. Provide code for a text link and some banner link alternatives, both with optimized keywords.

Support Us Page

The Support Us page includes a summary of all the ways in which people can support your site. You explicitly list these ways and provide reasons why the visitor may want to help out. The list can include supporting your site through monetary means—such as donating, buying your products or purchasing advertisement space. It can also involve requests for indirect support—for example, by asking the visitors to link to your site, write about it or vote for it.

---

*http://wordpress.org/plugins/printfriendly/

CHAPTER 21

Directories

Web directories are sites containing collections of links to other sites arranged into different categories. They differ from search engines in two ways. First, URLs are not gathered automatically but are instead submitted by site owners. Second, directories generally use human editors rather than automated software to review sites and decide if they will be included in the directory.

Submitting your site to web directories is an easy link building strategy, because anyone can submit and get listed. Directories can be of little use for the same reason. However, because it is a one-time affair, it is usually worth the effort. High quality directories provide one-way links which will help to increase your search rankings and may even bring in some traffic.

When submitting a site, web directories will ask for a brief description of the site, in addition to its URL and the category you want it placed in. Take some time writing this description in a way that concisely and accurately describes your site. Also make sure to select the most appropriate category for your site. This will increase the chance of your website being accepted into the directory.

Free Directories

There are thousands of directories on the web, but most of them either require you to pay an annual fee or are devalued link farms prevented from passing any search reputation. However, there are some directories that allow free submissions and that are worth submitting to. The largest of these is the Open Directory Project (dmoz.org). This is a volunteer-run directory with strong ties to Google. Submission to this directory is highly recommended. Below is a list of some other free directories.

- **Dmegs** – www.dmegs.com

- **ProLinkDirectory** – www.prolinkdirectory.com

- **SoMuch** – www.somuch.com

- **LdmStudio** – www.directory.ldmstudio.com

- **Wikiweb** – www.wikidweb.com

- **Jayde** – www.jayde.com
- **ExactSeek** – www.exactseek.com
- **PedstersPlanet** – www.pedsters-planet.co.uk
- **Infignos** – www.infignos.com

Paid Directories

Most high ranking directories require you to pay a fee, often a recurring one, to be included. Some of them charge you even for the privilege of being reviewed for inclusion. This is one instance where paying for PageRank does not get you into trouble. Still, you should not consider it unless your site has a strong monetization strategy in place. This way you can at least have the potential to earn more from the visitors referred than the yearly cost of submission.

How much a single paid directory link is worth in terms of search ranking, if any, can be difficult to track. If you are willing to try out a paid directory, then Yahoo's should be your first choice. The Yahoo Directory (dir.yahoo.com) is one of the biggest directories on the web, and one of the few directories that can provide traffic directly. Here is a list of some other large paid directories.

- **Business** – www.business.com
- **BestOfTheWeb** – www.botw.org
- **Ezilon** – www.ezilon.com
- **FamilyFriendlySites** – www.familyfriendlysites.com
- **V7Network** – directory.v7n.com
- **GoGuides** – www.goguides.org
- **AvivaDirectory** – www.avivadirectory.com

Besides general-purpose web directories, there are a large number of topical ones. If you can find one related to your niche that may provide a higher quality link than a link from a general directory. There are also many local and national web directories, which only accept links to sites from a particular region. These can be useful if your site is targeting a local or national audience only. Additionally, there are many RSS directories where you can add your RSS feed, if you have one. Promoting your feed in this way for people and other sites to use can result in some extra traffic.

Article Directories

An article directory allows you to submit content that will be released for free distribution and publication. In exchange, the directory allows you to include customizable dofollow back links in your article or in an author box. Below is a list of some of the largest article directories.

- **EzineArticles** – www.ezinearticles.com

- **Articlesbase** – www.articlesbase.com

- **Article Insider** – www.articleinsider.com

- **Article City** – www.articlecity.com

- **Article Dashboard** – www.articledashboard.com

- **Article Trader** – www.articletrader.com

- **Article Snatch** – www.articlesnatch.com

- **Article Alley** – www.articlealley.com

- **A1Articles** – www.a1articles.com

- **Buzzle** – www.buzzle.com

A high quality article has the potential to attract a lot of traffic to your site. The custom link can also provide significant search rankings for a key phrase of your choosing, since article directories are often highly ranked. Despite these advantages, spending time creating unique content for article directories is not recommended. That time is better spent creating content for your own site. What you want to do instead is to submit minor variations of the more popular text content you already have. By rewriting such an article slightly, it has a greater chance of being accepted into a manually approved article directory. It will also make sure that Google does not devalue the article and thereby your link. Content rewriting can be made easier using article spinning software, but the final proofreading will have to be done manually.

CHAPTER 22

Social Bookmarking

Social bookmarking involves submitting web addresses to bookmarking sites where people can find and visit them. On most such sites people vote on submitted pages, and the ones with the most votes are featured on the front page or on other top lists for a period of time.

The main benefit of bookmarking sites will be traffic and inbound links. You will be getting a one-way link on a high traffic site where you control the anchor text. A small percentage of the traffic sent from the bookmarking sites may also spread the link around to other sites and people if it is valuable or interesting enough.

Bookmarking Sites

Here is a list of some of the major social bookmarking sites.

- **Google bookmarks** – www.google.com/bookmarks
- **Digg** – www.digg.com
- **StumbleUpon** – www.stumbleupon.com
- **Del.icio.us** – www.delicious.com
- **Reddit** – www.reddit.com
- **Fark** – www.fark.com
- **Yahoo Bookmarks** – bookmarks.yahoo.com
- **Diigo** – www.diigo.com
- **Newsvine** – www.newsvine.com
- **Squidoo** – www.squidoo.com
- **Folkd** – www.folkd.com
- **Blinklist** – www.blinklist.com
- **Dropjack** – www.dropjack.com
- **CoRank** – www.corank.com

Submitting interesting content pages or link bait to the top social bookmarking sites can be a simple way to temporarily boost traffic to those pages. A time-saving online tool for this is Social Poster,* which allows you to automatically submit a page to all of the large social bookmarking and networking sites.

Getting to the Front Page

To receive large amounts of traffic from bookmarking sites, you need to reach their front page. On most social bookmarking sites, this can only be achieved within 24 hours of submitting a page. Within this time you need to receive a significant amount of votes to get on and stay on the front page.

If you submit a great piece of content you may reach the front page naturally. However, to reach it consistently you will need to give your submission an initial boost with the help of some bookmarking friends. These are people that agree to vote on each other every time one of them submits a post. Some 15 votes in the first hour after your submission should get the ball rolling. To reach the front page of Digg you may need as many as 50 votes within a couple of hours. In addition to having a great piece of content and receiving the initial votes, you will also need a catchy headline and a short well-thought out description that maximizes your click-through rate.

Keep in mind that the traffic spike will only last until your listing rolls off the front page and any other top lists. Social bookmarking traffic tends to have low conversion rates, so they may not earn you much money or provide many back links. Thus, I would not recommend spending too much time on these sites that could otherwise be spent on making content or directly marketing your site.

---

*http://www.socialposter.com

CHAPTER 23

Social Networking

Social networking sites refer to any community-driven site that allows social interactions and profile followers. This includes sites such as Twitter and Facebook. From the perspective of a web marketer, the purpose of social networking sites is to drive traffic to your website. They also provide a way to increase your search reputation, web presence, and credibility.

Register your Brand

Be preemptive and register your brand or site name on as many social networking sites as you can find, especially the popular ones in your niche. Even if you have no plans on becoming active on the sites, at least register there so you can reserve a username easily identifiable with your site. Also consider the added link value you get, as many social networking sites allow dofollow links in their profiles.

How to Get Traffic from Social Networks

There are four keys to getting traffic from social networking sites.

1. Post interesting content.
2. Post regularly.
3. Increase your number of followers.
4. Have a well-designed profile.

What to Post

The content you publish on social networks can be largely the same as what you publish in your newsletter or RSS feed if you have one. Basically, you post two kinds of content: promotional and non-promotional.

Your promotional content consists of short snippets encouraging readers to click through and read the full entry on your website or an affiliate website. Be sure to add a bit of context before you post the URL. That will increase the link's click-through rate and the post will not be mistaken for spam. Your website may already have a lot of interesting content that you can begin posting links to. To keep your profile fresh, post only one link at a time every day or so. This can help give new life to old content and drive new visitors and potential customers to your site.

Your non-promotional content refers to useful information and external links related to your niche that will be of interest to your followers. The key is balance. If you spend most of your time trying to promote your site or affiliate products, you are likely to alienate your followers and will not attract many new ones. On the other hand, if you make the profile useful to your readers it will attract more of them.

When to Update

As with all kinds of social sites, if you do not publish new content regularly, the traffic to your profile, and from there to your site, will slow down. If you are already publishing new content for your site, taking a few extra seconds to promote your content on social network sites is well worth the effort. Similarly, if you are already keeping up to date with all the latest developments in your niche—that is information that others will be interested in as well. So when you come across content that would be of interest to your readers, make sure to post it to your social network profiles.

How to Get Followers

Your social network profile serves the same purpose as your RSS feed and newsletter. It allows people to keep up to date with your site and with industry-related news by becoming *followers*—also known as *subscribers* or *friends*—of your profile. When you make a promotion to your site, a percentage of your followers will click through. Therefore, the more followers you have the more traffic you can expect to receive. For this reason, your followers are your major capital on social network sites.

The first thing you can do to attract followers is to invite your friends to join as your supporters. There is the issue of social proof on social network sites, where a profile with a lot of followers will draw others into it. Basically, if your followers have many followers, the chances are that some of these followers will notice you and will join your network as well, creating a snowball effect.

One way to attract more followers is to actively search for people on the network that have interests similar to what your site offers and invite them to join you. However, I do not recommend this method since it is a time consuming and roundabout approach for increasing your traffic. This brings up an important point. You do not want to spend time marketing your profile when you could be marketing your site directly. The profile should work for you, not the other way around. What you want to do instead is to set up ways to automatically attract followers—for example, by adding prominent buttons on your site inviting visitors to follow your profile. If they are already part of one of the networks you link to, they will be more likely to join you.

The Profile

Making your profile interesting is an important step in building a large set of followers. Be sure to pick a niche-targeted account name that is relevant to your brand and easy to remember. Your account name often becomes part of your profile's URL and may show up in searches.

Give your profile a professional design that is consistent with the website you are promoting. Provide background information about yourself and your site, and of course include your site URL in a prominent place. Be sure to make your profile public so that anyone can read it and follow you.

Social Networking Sites

Here is a list of some of the largest international social networking sites.

- **Facebook** – www.facebook.com
- **Twitter** – www.twitter.com
- **LinkedIn** – www.linkedin.com
- **Google Plus** – plus.google.com
- **Pinterest** – www.pinterest.com
- **Tumblr** – www.tumblr.com
- **Myspace** – www.myspace.com
- **LiveJournal** – www.livejournal.com
- **DeviantART** – www.deviantart.com

While posts can be made directly through the social networks' interfaces, to streamline things you can take advantage of tools to help you. For example, Twitter Feed* is a free online service that lets you link your RSS feed to both Twitter and Facebook. There are also WordPress plug-ins available for this task.

░ **Note**   Status Updater[+] – Allows you to publish content to Facebook and Twitter directly from your site.
Network Publisher[‡] – Lets you automatically publish posts to 5 out of 30 networks for free. A subscription is required to be able to post to more networks.

---

*http://twitterfeed.com
[+]http://wordpress.org/plugins/fb-status-updater/
[‡]http://wordpress.org/plugins/network-publisher/

Is It Worth your Time?

With any popular social networking site, you can invest a lot of time building a large network of targeted followers and supporters. However, if you are running an online business I do not recommend that you spend too much time there that could be spent making new content or directly promoting your site.

I advise you to try out social networking sites for at least a month, posting a snippet or two daily, to assess if they work for you. Your goal should be to get the most traffic from the least investment of time and effort. Social networking does not have to be interactive. You can just use it as a feed to broadcast information.

CHAPTER 24

PPC

Pay-Per-Click (PPC) is a paid form of advertising provided by search engines. It is the fastest way to drive large numbers of highly targeted visitors to your website. The principle is that you bid on keywords and then pay the search engine that amount every time a visitor clicks on your ad. Your ad then appears on the search engine result pages or on websites relevant to yours that are affiliated with the search engine.

Many webmasters have spent years building and marketing their sites, and still do not come close to the flow of visitors that a PPC campaign can generate in a matter of hours. However, even if you plan to run a PPC campaign, do not forget to do all the basic things that will help you get traffic for free.

A PPC campaign is an efficient marketing solution because costs are strictly controlled and adverts precisely targeted. PPC gives you the flexibility to display a variety of advert formats and even target your ads to specific languages and geographic locations. You get all of this and you are only charged if people click on your ads – meaning every dollar of your budget works towards harnessing new potential customers.

PPC Is Not for Everyone

Buying visitors is only a viable strategy if you earn more money than you spend. It is therefore a strategy mainly useful for e-commerce sites or Content/e-commerce sites. A content only site relying mainly on advertisement income is unlikely to earn enough revenue per visitor to make the transaction profitable.

Choosing a PPC Provider

The first part of setting up a PPC campaign is deciding where you want your adverts to appear. At present the top international PPC providers are Google AdWords* and Yahoo Advertising.† Other big names in the PPC market include: Bing Ads, MIVA, and Marchex. Doing private ad deals with other site owners and companies is another option.

---

*http://adwords.google.com
†http://advertising.yahoo.com

Google AdWords

Google AdWords is the biggest PPC provider. The registration is free and you only pay for clicks. Clicks can cost as little as $0.01, but some highly competitive keywords can cost upwards of $10 or more.

Your purchased ads are displayed above and to the right of the normal search results, under the sponsored links sections. Adverts can also appear on search sites within Google's Search Network, which includes AOL Search, Ask.com, and Netscape. Additionally, adverts can appear on relevant websites that have joined Google's AdSense program.

Determining a Visitor's Worth

When you pay for visitors to your site, it is essential that you have optimized the site for converting visitors into customers. If your site is not converting, then you have internal issues to handle first. Before you even think about a PPC campaign, you need to calculate the average income you earn from every visitor. The formula is simply:

- Average income / Average number of visitors = Income per visitor

For example, if you earn on average $250 from 1000 visitors, then your average income per visitor is $0.25. Therefore, in order to make a profit in this example the average cost per click for the product keywords needs to be less than $0.25. If you determine that your income per visitor is larger than the cost per visitor for your targeted keywords, go ahead and make a test run with Google AdWords.

Bear in mind that different traffic sources have different conversion rates. PPC traffic generally has a higher conversion rate than other traffic types—typically around 2 to 3 times higher than search engine traffic. This is because PPC allows you to target keywords that signal buying intent. Therefore, even if your income per visitor is a bit lower than your cost per visitor, you may still want to try out a PPC campaign.

Advert Campaign

When starting an AdWords PPC campaign, you get to create your own advert units and select for which keywords the units will be displayed. You also get to set a daily budget and the maximum cost per click. These settings will be explored further below.

Advert Units

AdWords allows for a variety of different ad types—including text, image, and video ads. To keep things simple, you should start with a text ad. The elements that make up a text ad are the headline, the description and the destination URL. You want to focus on optimizing only the ad text and the headline.

New York Budget Hotel
Clean and close to subway.
Students save 20%!
www.example.com

Example of an AdWords text ad

With PPC it is undesirable to pay for untargeted visitors who will not buy anything. The ad unit should therefore be designed to eliminate window shoppers, while still attracting the target audience. It needs to be optimized to qualify the reader and not for the highest click-through rate. For this reason, the ad description and headline must describe exactly what you offer. The reader should know without going to the website whether the product is for them or not.

Though you do not want to optimize for a high click-through rate, you also do not want your CTR to be too low. This is because Google will punish a bad click-through rate with a low quality score, placing your ad lower on the search result pages and making you pay more per click.

To find the best combination of headline and text, you need to experiment by creating a number of different advert units. You can start with a basic ad unit that simply states your product or service offer. From this basic ad unit you then make additional ad units that vary in only the one variable you want to test. For example, you can try adding a guarantee, a benefit, a keyword phrase, a limited offer, a call to action or a price to your ad description. Be sure that all ad units send the customer directly to an offer-specific sales page dedicated to closing the sale.

Advert Keywords

After deciding on your ad units, the next step is to decide for which keywords your ads will appear. A keyword phrase can be specified using any one of these four keyword matching options: broad, phrase, exact, and negative match. The first three were described in the Keyword Research chapter. The last one, negative match, is specified by prefixing the keyword with a minus sign (-). It can be used to prevent your adverts from appearing when a user searches for something that is unlikely to result in a sale.

1. **Broad match** – The ad will show for similar phrases and relevant variations – e.g. keyword.

2. **Phrase match** – The ad shows for search terms that include this exact phrase – e.g. "keyword".

3. **Exact match** – The ad shows for this exact search term – e.g. [keyword].

4. **Negative match** – The ad will not show if this search term occurs – e.g. -keyword.

To find keywords for your product, visit the Google AdWords Keyword Planner once again. Use this tool to create a list of keywords that are relevant to your product and have very low ad competition, as listed by this tool. This will bring in targeted visitors while you pay as little as possible per click. You should try many variations of the keywords people may use when looking for anything related to your product. You may also like to include plurals, abbreviations, and different word orders in your keyword list. Make sure that each keyword phrase appears on a separate line. This will make it easy to import the list into Google AdWords.

Advert Budget

In addition to ad units and keywords, you can set the daily budget for your campaign. The budget specifies how much you will spend on AdWords advertising each day. You want to start small to see if the campaign is profitable. Provided that you earn more money than you spend, you can keep on increasing the budget more and more. The more money you spend, the more money you can make. Keep in mind that the larger your daily budget becomes, the more important it is that you monitor your campaign carefully. Since you bid on the keywords against lots of competitors, the cost-per-click can vary greatly, especially in highly profitable niches. It is essential that you do not pay more per visitor than you earn in return.

Another important setting is the maximum cost per click (CPC) bid. This is the highest price you are willing to pay for someone to click on your ad. It can be set globally for a campaign or ad group, as well as for specific keywords you advertise for. This keyword budget will be used to automatically bid on ad placements against competing bidders. Even if there is no competition, the ad will not be free. The minimum CPC is determined by an AdWords quality score.* Every keyword in your campaign has a quality score associated with it. The score can be displayed by adding the "Qual. score" column from the campaign's Keywords page. Your account as a whole also has a hidden quality score that comes from the average of all individual keywords' quality scores.

The most important attribute for raising your quality score is to have a high click-through rate (CTR). Only the CTR on Google Search matters and what will be considered a good CTR varies for different keywords. Another quality attribute is to use ad units that are relevant to the keywords in that ad group. To get a higher quality score, you want each keyword to also appear in your ad copy. For this to be possible, you should create several tightly focused ad groups. One more factor is the quality of the landing page.† In addition to having credibility indicators on the page, you want the keywords you bid for to also appear on the landing page. All in all, there are more than 100 factors affecting the quality score and not all of them are disclosed. However, those mentioned here are considered the most important ones.

By setting a high maximum CPC bid you can have your ad appear for more expensive keywords and locations, which may result in higher conversion rates. On the other hand, a low maximum CPC bid can bring in more traffic for your daily budget, provided that

---

*https://support.google.com/adwords/answer/2454010
†https://support.google.com/adwords/answer/2404197

you can find keywords with little to no competition. To estimate the amount of traffic you will receive for a given CPC, daily budget, and keyword list, you can use Google's Traffic Estimator.*

Advert Tracking

Once your campaign is set up, AdWords will begin to bid for and show your ad units automatically. To be able to track your paid traffic separately from your free traffic, you want to link your AdWords account[†] to your Google Analytics account. Statistics will then begin to appear in the AdWords section of your Analytics account. During testing, you may want to configure your campaign to rotate your ads evenly,[‡] instead of only showing the ones that yield the most clicks. You also want to set up conversion tracking[§] from your Analytics account, to be able to track which keywords and ad units convert the most. This involves placing a tracking script on the page that appears after a purchase has been made, typically the Thank You page.

With your tracking set up, you will begin to see which keywords and ad units perform the best by earning you the most. Once that becomes apparent, you want to dedicate your budget towards those ad units and keywords. Keywords that do not perform well can be removed from your list while you add more keywords similar to those that are performing. Based on the ad units that convert the most, you can create a new set of ads that includes the best performing elements of the successful ad units. As you find your PPC campaign becoming optimized, you can raise your daily budget and tweak your CPC further to bring in ever more targeted traffic.

---

*https://adwords.google.com/select/TrafficEstimatorSandbox
†https://support.google.com/adwords/answer/3207171
‡https://support.google.com/adwords/answer/112876
§https://support.google.com/analytics/answer/1032415

PART 4

Monetization

CHAPTER 25

Profit

A high traffic website is a powerful asset. It can become an automated money-making machine that works for you 24 hours per day, 365 days per year without pay—a business system that generates money, whether you work or not. It is a truly incredible system for generating cash flow.

Keys to Making Money Online

The three keys to making money from a website are:

1. **Traffic** – The more visitors you have the more you stand to make from any monetization strategy.

2. **Value** – No matter how many visitors you have, if your site does not have captivating content people will not stay on your site, let alone earn you any money.

3. **Monetizing strategies** – The right combination of income strategies is essential to maximizing your profit.

Monetization Strategies

There are five ways to monetize a site: **donations**, **advertising**, **affiliate programs**, **services**, and **products**. These strategies will be discussed in detail in the chapters to come. Which strategies are most suitable for your site depends on its type. Generally, there are the following two combinations:

- **Content site** – Advertising, affiliate programs and donations.

- **E-commerce site** – Selling products or services while running affiliate programs and ad campaigns.

Professional e-commerce sites generally do not have advertising or accept donations, because it diminishes their credibility, which in turn reduces sales. Likewise, they do not join other sites' affiliate programs, because they make a greater profit from selling their own products and running their own affiliate program.

For a content site credibility is less of an issue, because it is not trying to sell the visitor anything. It can therefore make full use of the other income sources—advertising, affiliate programs, and donations.

A content/e-commerce site can successfully make use of all five monetization strategies, but not on the same pages. The sales pages should only derive income from selling products and services, while the content pages can earn money from advertising, affiliate programs, and donations.

Income Comparison

Selling products and services are undoubtedly the most profitable income strategies in terms of income per visitor. A well optimized e-commerce site can earn anywhere in the range of 10-100 times the income of a content site per visitor. However, a content site, utilizing affiliate and advertising income, does have a much easier time attracting visitors. Therefore, a well marketed, quality content site has the potential to earn just as much money as an e-commerce site. As for donations, this is a poor monetization strategy at best.

CHAPTER 26

Donations

The first and easiest monetization strategy is to accept donations. If you provide quality content for free you can allow people to support your work in this way. You simply embed a donation button onto a clearly visible section of your website. The most common method of accepting donations online is through PayPal.* Another interesting way to receive donations is through the micro donation system Flattr.†

Increasing Donations

To increase the amount of donations you receive, be sure to give people a reason for donating, by explaining how the money will be used. You can also include a progress bar that displays how much money you have received, and how much more you will need to reach a set goal. Make sure to ask for donations in prominent locations on your site.

Evaluation

As you may expect this monetization strategy provides the least amount of cash flow and the income is very sporadic. Unless you are running a charity site or have traffic levels like Wikipedia, I advise you not to spend too much time trying to get people to donate, and instead focus your efforts on other more profitable monetization strategies.

---

*https://www.paypal.com/cgi-bin/webscr?cmd=p/xcl/rec/donate-intro-outside
†http://www.flattr.com

CHAPTER 27

Advertising

Advertising is the second strategy you can use to monetize your site. Including advertisements on your site is a simple way to derive an income from it. Ads can come in the form of text ads, banner ads, link ads, feed ads or video ads. The most popular web advertising service is Google AdSense.* Other providers include: CrispAds, AdBrite, Chikita, Kontera, BlogAds, ValueClick media, Tribal Fusion, Text Link Brokers, and Text Link Ads. You also have the option of doing private ad deals with other websites or companies.

Google AdSense

Google AdSense is a free service that provides text, image, and video ads that are automatically chosen to match the content on your pages. With its online relevancy matching, the AdSense platform has no close rival.

You get paid when someone clicks on your ads. How much you earn per click depends on how much advertisers have bid for your keywords by using the Google AdWords[†] service. Each click may pay you anything from $0.01 to $10, or even more in profitable niches. You can get some idea of how much clicks are worth in your niche with the Google AdWords Traffic Estimator.[‡]

In addition to including AdSense in your content, you can also earn money by adding AdSense to your website's search, your mobile site and to any videos you may have.

Note   Quick AdSense[§] – This plug-in provides a flexible way to insert Google AdSense code into a WordPress site.

---

*https://www.google.com/adsense/
†https://adwords.google.com
‡https://adwords.google.com/select/TrafficEstimatorSandbox
§http://wordpress.org/plugins/quick-adsense/

AdSense Income

There are three factors that govern how much money you earn from AdSense.

- **Click-through rate (CTR)** – The percentage of visitors that actually click on your ads. Average click-through rates can vary greatly, from as low as 0.5% to as high as 10% or more.

- **Revenue per click** – The percentage of the cost per click (CPC) paid out to publishers is 68% for content ads and 51% for search ads. For other AdSense services the percentages vary and they are not disclosed by Google.

- **Page impressions** – Average number of page views for a period of time.

Using these terms, the formula for AdSense earnings is simply:

- Click-through rate * Revenue per click * Page impressions per day = Income per day

For example, if you have 100 content pages, each receiving 100 page views per day, you would have 100x100 = 10 000 daily page impressions. With an average CTR of 1%, paying an average of $0.50 per click, you have an income of 10 000 * 0.01 * 0.50 = $50 per day, or $1500 per month.

Increasing Revenue Per Click

Here are some tips on how to increase the payment you receive per AdSense click.

- **Higher paying keywords** – By writing keyword-specific content pages for high paying keywords within your site's niche, you will earn more money for each click.

- **Focused content** – The more focused your content pages are, the better Google can determine which ads are most relevant to your readers. This in turn increases the chance that someone will click on them.

- **First ad** – The first AdSense ad displayed in your site's HTML will contain the highest paying ads. Aim to position this ad where you have the highest click-through rate.

Increasing Click-Through Rate

There are various ways of tricking users into clicking ads, but that does not give a good user experience. Techniques such as pop-ups and blinking ads can severely undermine a site's credibility and likability, and it is not worth using them. Some far less annoying ways of increasing your CTR will be covered here.

AdSense Formats

AdSense offers a variety of ad formats. All things being equal, the relative click-through rate of these formats is different, as can be seen in the diagram below.

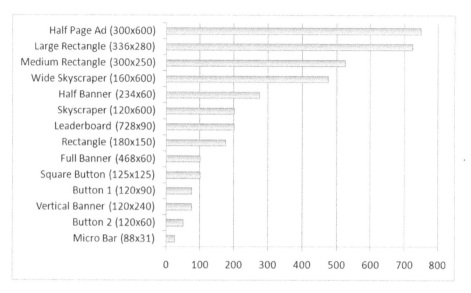

Relative click-through rates for various AdSense formats. Source: DoubleClick.com

In short, larger ad formats typically outperform smaller formats. Similarly, wider formats have a higher click-through rate than their taller counterparts. Keep in mind that while such ad formats tend to perform well, they may not always fit the best with your site design.

AdSense Positioning

You want to place the ads where they get the visitors' attention without annoying them. AdSense ads can be displayed anywhere on your site, but certain positions are better than others. The following heat map shows locations where visitors are more likely to see them and therefore more likely to click on them. The colors fade from dark-gray (strongest performance) to white (weakest performance).

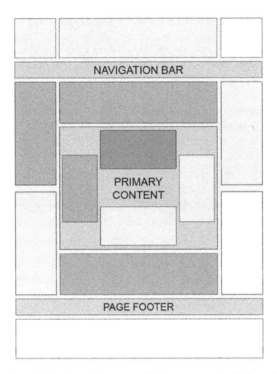

A heat map showing which ad positions are likely to generate higher click-through rates. Source: Google AdSense

The top left of the content is one of the highest performing areas together with the main content on the page. Integrating ads into the content often gives the highest click-through rates.

Ads placed near navigational aids also usually do well, because many users will focus on these areas when they are ready to navigate to another page. For the same reason, ads below the content will perform well, provided that your content is good enough to keep the visitor reading. The end of the content is a natural stopping point where the visitor is ready to click to go somewhere else.

Another good spot is right above the content. Most visitors will naturally see this ad and thus are more likely to click on it. In general, ads that show up above the fold perform better than ads below the fold. However, be sure not to crowd out the content with too many ads above the fold. If a reader arrives at your site and has to scroll to see the content, they are more likely to leave right away.

To track your results, be sure to create separate AdSense channels for every ad location. This way you can see how each ad performs.

Ad Integration

Savvy Internet users will not even look at anything that looks like an advertisement, a concept known as banner blindness. The key to overcoming this and getting people to pay attention to ads is to make them appear less like ads and more like content. By making the advert appear to be part of the content you can improve your click-through rate significantly. Here are some suggestions on how to achieve this.

1. **Content inlining** – Wrapping text around the ad makes it appear to be part of the content.

2. **Alignment** – Positioning the ad on the same line as content will make it look less like an ad.

3. **Style blending** – The ad should use the same font and color as the rest of the site with a transparent background and no borders.

4. **Repetition** – Including text ads near text links and banner ads near images is an effective method of integrating ads with content.

5. **Random placement** – Inserting ads randomly into the content can help defeat banner blindness.

Ad Quantity

Google allows you to place up to 3 ad units, 3 link units, and 2 AdSense search boxes on each page. However, displaying this many ads on a single page is seldom appropriate. How many ads you want to display depends on the amount of content a page has and the overall site design. Sites that have too many ads appear spammy and unprofessional. As a result of this, they may attract fewer visitors and thus earn less revenue, not more.

Ad Blocking

Ad blockers are browser extensions that block advertisements from showing up in the user's browser. The most popular one is Adblock Plus,* a Firefox extension. Chrome and IE similarly have their own ad block extensions. A comprehensive study performed in 2012 by ClarityRay† showed that 9.26% of Internet users in US and Europe use ad-blockers. These blockers are most common for web users of technology and news sites.

Ad blocking is a very controversial issue, since most websites rely primarily on advertisements for their income. One strategy, which for example Google uses, is to not bother ad-blocking visitors in any way. They are after all still a minority, and there are many other ways of making money online.

---

*https://addons.mozilla.org/en-US/firefox/addon/1865/
†http://www.clarityray.com

If your site relies heavily on ad income, you can use JavaScript to display a message only for ad-blocking visitors. The message can for example contain a polite request for the visitor to donate, subscribe or to disable the ad block software for your site. This notification commonly takes the form of an image that replaces the blocked ads, or a discrete pop-up message.

Note   Anti-AdBlock* – This WP plug-in displays a customizable one-time message for regular ad blocking visitors.

---

*http://wordpress.org/plugins/anti-adblock/

CHAPTER 28

Affiliates

The third monetization strategy is affiliate programs. Similar to web advertising, as an affiliate you include a link on your site to your affiliate partner's site. However, this link takes the visitor directly to a page selling a product or service. If the visitor purchases the item, you earn a referral fee, often a percentage of the item's cost. Affiliate programs generally pay on a cost-per-action (CPA) basis, where visitors need to take some action—such as making a purchase or signing up for a service—before you earn any revenue.

Essentially, affiliate programs allow you to earn money by selling other people's products and services. Some of the largest affiliate programs include Amazon Associates,* eBay Partner Network,† and ClickBank.‡ You can also look through an affiliate directory—such as Affiliate Scout§ or Associate Programs‖—to find an affiliate vendor that suits your site's niche closely.

Amazon Affiliate

Amazon Associates is the largest online affiliate marketing program and also one of the first. It is free to join and easy to integrate with your site. In contrast to contextual advertising, you do not just put a piece of code into a template. Rather you pick and choose which items you want to help sell, and then add affiliate links to those items from your site's pages.

Amazon is a good affiliate program to start with, not only because of its wide range of products but also because it is a trusted site where people spend a lot of money.

Getting Paid

The commission rate on Amazon starts at 4% for most products, and there is a sliding scale where the more you sell the higher your commission goes. See their compensation page for details.¶ You earn a commission on everything a person buys within 24 hours of you sending them to Amazon, not just on the product that you send people to.

---

*https://affiliate-program.amazon.com
†https://www.ebaypartnernetwork.com
‡http://www.clickbank.com
§http://www.affiliatescout.com
‖http://www.associateprograms.com
¶https://affiliate-program.amazon.com/gp/associates/join/compensation.html

Affiliate Payment Models

As mentioned earlier, affiliate programs commonly pay a referral fee when a purchase is made—a so-called *one-time commission*. Some sites though, particularly those that sell subscription services, may offer lifetime commissions. That is, their affiliate program will pay you a recurring fee for as long as the referred customer stays with the service. Though the conversion rate for services is often lower than it is for products, the long term value of such a customer makes these affiliate programs very profitable, provided that you can find a good one in your niche.

Most affiliate programs—such as Amazon Associates—are one-tier, where you get paid for the purchases or sign-ups made by the people you refer. In a two-tier program, you also earn a commission on everything the referred person earns through the program if they too decide to join it. With multi-tier programs, this continues even further down the line. This allows you to earn an income not only by selling other people's products and services, but also by promoting their affiliate programs.

Increasing Affiliate Sales

There are many techniques you can use to increase the sales of your affiliate products. Below is a list of the more ethical ones.

1. **Relevance** – Identify products that are relevant not only to the site's niche, but also to the subject of the content page promoting it.

2. **Value** – Choose products that you fully believe will benefit your visitors.

3. **Quality** – Pick products with good reputations and professional sales pages.

4. **Quantity** – Promoting a single product on a page often yields better results than trying to promote several on the same page.

5. **Context** – Affiliate links well integrated into content do better than links in sidebars.

6. **Honesty** – Give an open and honest appraisal of the product, including both its strengths and weaknesses.

7. **Incentive** – Offer something that adds value to the product if it is bought through your affiliate link.

8. **Trust** – If you have consistently helped people and been useful to them, they are more likely to respond to your recommendations.

Affiliate Link Placements

Affiliate links cannot only be included on your site. They can just as well be placed in your newsletters, e-mails, e-books or any other e-products that you create. Including your affiliate links on social media sites is another possibility, though you want to be careful not to spam people. Often, linking to a content page on your site that contains the affiliate link is a better idea than posting the affiliate link directly. As with every other money-making strategy, affiliate marketing can be used both ethically and unethically. It is recommended that you disclose the use of affiliate links, for example, by using a link tooltip.

```
<a href="affiliate-url" title="[Affiliate link]
Product Title">Product Title</a>
```

Your Own Affiliate Program

If you have a good product you can offer an affiliate program of your own. This way you can allow other site owners to promote your product in exchange for a percentage of any resulting sales. Because there is a financial benefit for your links to be promoted, your affiliate partners will have incentive to sell your product.

Affiliate marketing helps reduce unnecessary sales costs, bring in more potential customers and make more sales with less time and effort. With software tools it is possible not only to automate your sales process, but also to automate the management, tracking, and payments of the affiliate program—thereby eliminating your costs of sales and making negative cash flow through your program impossible.

This monetization strategy has incredible leverage, in that your revenue has the potential to grow exponentially. One affiliate can lead to more and so on, until you have hundreds and possibly thousands of motivated salesmen promoting your product or service—far more than you could ever afford with a traditional sales model.

Recruiting Affiliates

The best place to start recruiting affiliates is within your own website. A simple "Join our Affiliate Program" page on your site is the ideal starting point. Getting a listing in an affiliate directory is another quick and easy way to generate interest in your program. You can also e-mail webmasters in your niche and ask them if they want to promote your product through your affiliate program. In addition to commissions, you may want to give the webmaster other incentives, such as promoting their site or product in return, or by creating a special affiliate offer just for them. Once you have a good affiliate program in place and have gotten the word out, you may find that potential affiliates will start to actively seek you out without any need for recruitment on your part.

CHAPTER 29

Services

Selling services is the fourth monetization strategy. A service is an intangible product that you "rent out" rather than sell. There are two types: manual and automated.

Manual Services

A *manual service* is one where you trade your time and expertise for a one-time fee. Once you have established yourself as an expert in your niche, you can start to earn money by offering a variety of services related to that area. Though this is not a passive monetization strategy, it can yield a substantial side income while you work on building your passive income streams.

If you want to try out selling services, then start making a list of what services you can offer from your site. Preferably, find ones that are in high demand and require specialized skill, so that you can charge a large fee for them to make it worth your while. Here are some examples of services:

- **Consulting** – You can offer consulting services to other people or businesses that could use your expertise.

- **Writing services** – Guest writing, professional blogging, proofreading or sponsored reviews.

- **Web services** – Graphic design, template design, web development, or website creation.

- **Public speaking** – Speaking at events or holding seminars.

- **Support** – Allow people to contact you personally for support related to your site or products.

When you have found out what services you want to offer, add a "Hire me" page to your site that informs visitors of what services you provide. You can also sell your services through eBay and other similar sites.

Automated Services

Certain types of services can be *automated*. Basically, you program a piece of software (or construct a machine) that replaces the work of a human in one area. Instead of selling the software or machine, you allow people to use it for a period of time by paying a fee. Examples of this would be online tools for keyword research or link analysis.

Another type of automated service is where you own something of value that can be rented out through an automated system. The most common example of this in the online world is where you allow people to purchase advertising space on your site, for instance with Google AdSense. Another example is the server resources that web hosting companies rent out.

A third type of automation is a subscription service of some sort—for example, paid memberships, where you allow subscribed visitors to access exclusive content or other special features. The key to a successful subscription service is to offer a consistent flow of value that your subscribers cannot find anywhere else. Providing an exclusive community environment for the subscribers is another important component.

The main benefit of owning a paid automated service is that it provides you with a monthly income from each subscribed customer. As long as a customer remains subscribed to the service, they will keep earning you money. This in contrast to the one-time fee you would receive from selling the automated service as a product. Though the monthly fee may have to be low to stay competitive, the long-term value of each customer is great. Negative aspects include that it is often harder to get a visitor to sign up for a recurring fee than to buy something for a one-time fee. There may also be significant competition from free alternatives to your service.

CHAPTER 30

Products

Selling products is the fifth monetization strategy. In contrast to most of the previously discussed monetization strategies, the strategy of developing your own product can take a significant amount of time and effort. Still, it is perhaps the most profitable monetization strategy because of the leverage it provides.

The exact type of product you want to develop depends on your site's niche, as well as on your own special skills and knowledge. Obviously, the more you know about your chosen field, the more likely you are to create a successful product that appeals to people in that field. I recommend that you brainstorm some 20 product ideas before narrowing them down to a single one. While products can be virtually anything, they can be divided into two distinct categories: digital and physical.

Digital Products

Digital products have a lot of advantages over physical products. They do not need to be manufactured, stored or shipped. Therefore, virtually all overhead and production costs are eliminated. It is only data, and data costs nothing to replicate and transfer. Even so they have a high perceived value. Digital products can be downloaded after payment and the end-user can enjoy their benefits immediately.

Producing digital products can be fairly simple and inexpensive. In particular, information products tend to sell well and have high profit margins. They are also difficult for competitors to duplicate. If you have an informational content site, then you already have the content on which you can base your product. Below is a list of the main digital information products that you can produce from content.

- **EBook** – Compile the best of your site into an eBook and send it in for copy editing and proofreading.

- **ABook** – Have a professional create an audio program based on your eBook.

- **Video seminar** – Hold a seminar based on content from your site. Record it professionally and produce a video seminar from it.

- **Video tutorials** – Instructional content can be made into video tutorials.

- **ECourse** – A set of lessons in various media formats compiled from your other informational products.

Physical Products

Products made up of atoms have some drawbacks compared to digital products. Foremost, getting a physical product from idea into the customer's hands often involves a lot more steps. Fortunately, all steps from production to shipping and support can be delegated to companies that specialize in such services.

One popular company that specializes in this is CafePress.* This is an online retailer that produces user-customized merchandise—such as clothing and posters. You provide the designs or slogans for the products you choose to sell, and they produce and ship them for you. You pay nothing for the service since the products are only produced after you sell them. Other similar retailers include Zazzle† and Printfection.‡

The informational products discussed previously can just as easily be packaged and sold as hardware—such as books, CDs, and DVDs. They can be manufactured cheaply through online publishers such as CreateSpace,§ which is Amazon's publishing company. This allows you to sell the products on trusted ecommerce sites—such as eBay and Amazon—in addition to your own site. Through CreateSpace you can distribute your product not only to Amazon.com, but also to other online retailers as well as bookstores, libraries, and schools.

Physical products have one significant advantage over digital products. People are more accustomed to paying for them than for data bits. It is simply easier to get a person to pay for a T-shirt than for a piece of data.

Market Demand Research

Be sure to research whether there is a demand for the product you plan to create. The simplest way of determining this is to see if others are selling similar products successfully. You can discover this using the Google AdWords Keyword Planner once again. This time, add the column for Approximate CPC (cost per click) and search for your product category. Note that you need to be logged in with your AdWords account for this option to be available. If people are paying more than $0.10 for keywords in and around your product niche, you can be fairly certain your product will have a market. The more people are willing to pay per click, the more profitable the niche will be. Additionally, you can use Google Trends‖ to see if your product category is rising or falling in popularity.

---

*http://www.cafepress.com
†http://www.zazzle.com
‡http://www.printfection.com
§https://www.createspace.com
‖http://www.google.com/trends

Product Marketing

The steps so far have been to determine what you want to sell and finding out if there is a sufficient market for it. Once that has been established you want to automate the process of getting the product into the customers' hands. Then, the final step is to market your product. This attribute of products—that you can market them directly—is a significant advantage over the advertisement and affiliate income strategies.

On a content site you market the site itself since you cannot market your ads or affiliate links. This is an indirect method and therefore has a low conversion rate. On an e-commerce site, however, you can market your products directly. You not only earn a much larger income per conversion, but you can also achieve a much higher conversion rate.

When the time comes to start promoting your product, you want to have a market strategy in place. Start by researching other successful websites that sell similar products and see what tactics they employ. By finding out how they are promoting their products, you will be able to duplicate much of their success.

To give some examples, one method of promotion is to sell your product on eBay and Amazon. This will make your product visible for people searching through their search engines. Another method is to hire popular bloggers and people with influence to write favorable reviews about your product. There is also the possibility of distributing demos of your product on P2P networks to increase awareness. Additionally, the link building strategies discussed in previous chapters work just as well for sales pages as for content pages. The tactic of buying traffic through PPC is another great promotion tactic.

PART 5

Conversions

CHAPTER 31

Stickiness

A sticky website is one where a visitor arrives and finds it difficult to leave. This is of vital importance to the success of your online business. There is no point in bringing visitors to your site if they instantly leave.

Besides getting traffic to your site, you need to know how to keep your visitors there and how to make them return for more. These two concepts are closely related. The more time people spend on your site the more likely they are to become repeat visitors and to earn you money.

How Long are Visitors Staying

With Google Analytics* set up for your site you can see detailed statistics on how long visitors are staying at your site. From the Analytics website click to view the report for your site. Then navigate to Audience ➤ Overview and display the Average Time on Site graph. This graph will show you how your site's stickiness has changed over time and if you are heading in the right direction.

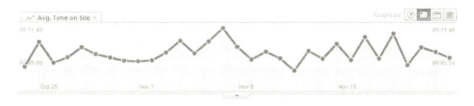

Example of a Time on Site trend

Another interesting metric related to stickiness is the bounce rate graph, which you can also find under the Audience ➤ Overview page. The bounce rate is the percentage of visitors who leave your site after only a single page view. The average bounce rate is around 50%. Anything more than that and you may need to work on improving your site's stickiness. The Pages/Visit graph is also of interest. The more pages your visitors view, the more stickiness your site has.

---

*http://www.google.com/analytics

How to Keep Visitors at your Site Longer

Making a site sticky involves several aspects, many of which have already been discussed. In short, the main key is to consistently offer a large amount of easily accessible high quality value that is relevant to your visitor's interests within your site's niche. If you can do this, your visitors will keep coming back to you again and again and will stay long. Value here represents either content, products, services or a combination of these three elements. In addition to having value, your site as a whole needs to be likable. It needs to have a high quality design, fast page load time, easy navigation, and be validated to provide a pleasant user experience.

Hook the Visitor

From the Audience ➤ Behaviour ➤ Engagement page you can see how long visitors stay on your site on average. You may find that a large percentage of your visitors are only staying 0-10 seconds. These visitors did not reach the hook point, where they decide to stay rather than go somewhere else.

The first thing the visitors see when they arrive at your site needs to hook them so that they will not instantly leave the site. They need to know immediately that they have arrived at the right page—at a page providing them with what they are looking for, whether it is information, entertainment, products or services. The content needs to be focused and interesting enough to maintain their attention long enough for them to reach this point.

For a text content page, the first thing the visitor should see is the headline. This is the piece of text that, if interesting enough, will get the visitor to read the first sentence. The first sentence will get them to read the first paragraph, which will get them to read the rest of the content. Once they have read the page, if they are sufficiently hooked, they may explore other related pages on your site. The final step is when the visitor becomes a return visitor or loyal customer. Anywhere along the way, you can lose the visitor if you bore them with something other than what they want.

Linking Structure

A key concept in making a site sticky is to create a dense link structure throughout your site. Each page is another way to keep visitors staying longer on your site. Going beyond easy navigation menus, you want to give visitors many ways to explore the other parts of your site. If a visitor traverses your site only to find more and more interesting content, they are more likely to become a return visitor of your site. The most clicked on links on a page are those placed within the content. Therefore, it is a good idea to include content links whenever appropriate to other related pages within your site.

Related Pages

Additional relevant links can be placed so they are clearly visible just below the content, so that once the visitor has finished reading the current page they will be exposed to even more interesting content. This can draw their attention to other content that is similar to what attracted them in the first place and get them to explore more than one page.

⬚ **Note** Yet Another Related Posts* – This WP plug-in allows you to display a list of pages contextually related to the current page.

Sequential Pages

Going one step further than including links to related content, you can organize your content pages into series of related pages that can be traversed like chapters in a book. For such a series, be sure to include next/previous navigation links back and forth within the series.[†] Also add a chapter list or table of contents that tells the visitor where he is in the current series.

Popular Pages

Highlight the best content your site has to offer by featuring a "Best of" or "Most viewed" section on your site. These links should be placed in a sidebar instead of in the content area, since they are not related to the current page.

⬚ **Note** WordPress Popular Posts[‡] – This plug-in displays the most popular posts on your site.

Other similar sidebar sections you may want to include are Recent posts[§] and Recent comments.[‖]

Interesting Links

In addition to positioning your links in places where they are more likely to be seen, there are a number of other ways to increase their click-through rate. The key is to attract the visitor's attention and then to get them interested enough to click the link. A well thought out anchor text is a good start. This can be combined with an interesting image that you have associated with each page. The clickable image can be positioned to the left of the link in places where you have a bit more space, such as in the sidebar or after the content. A third technique to increase the click-through rate is to place a line or two of preview text under the link, ending with another link for reading the rest of the content.

---

*http://wordpress.org/plugins/yet-another-related-posts-plugin/
†http://codex.wordpress.org/Next_and_Previous_Links
‡http://wordpress.org/plugins/wordpress-popular-posts/
§http://wordpress.org/plugins/recent-posts-plugin/
‖http://wordpress.org/plugins/recent-comments-plugin/

CHAPTER 32

Return Visitors

Returning visitors usually account for the majority of the traffic to a successful well established website. These visitors are more valuable to you, because the more time they spend at your site the more likely they are to earn you money through your monetization strategies. An added benefit of return visitors is that they are easier to convert into paying customers, because they have established trust with your site.

Getting people to come back to your site is a similar challenge to getting people to stay there for long periods of time. Therefore, the strategies discussed in the previous chapter on Stickiness will also increase the likelihood of your visitors becoming returning visitors. This chapter will focus on another powerful strategy for attracting return visitors, namely subscriptions.

Subscriptions

If you are running a regularly updated site, it is a good idea to let visitors subscribe to those updates. This will increase your number of return visitors significantly. Whenever you release new content your subscribers will be informed, sending a percentage of them returning to your site. There are three main ways in which you can allow visitors to follow updates on your site: RSS feeds, email newsletters and social networks.

RSS Feeds

An RSS (Rich Site Summary) feed is a mechanism to distribute content from a site out to many readers. This allows visitors subscribed to the feed to get instant notification of updates. RSS feeds are not read directly. Instead, they are read through feed readers—such as Feedly for Firefox.*

Most CMS, including WordPress, already have RSS feeds integrated for posts and comments.† You simply need to add a link to your post feed in one or more prominent places on your site. Preferably, the link should use the standard RSS feed icon so people can find it easily.

---

*https://addons.mozilla.org/en-us/firefox/addon/feedly/
†http://codex.wordpress.org/WordPress_Feeds

RSS feed icon

To make using the RSS feed simpler, you can add a subscribe link that takes the visitor directly to a feed reader, for example, using a Google Reader subscription button.* If you are interested in keeping track of how many RSS subscribers you have, the feed can be linked through Google's FeedBurner service.†

░ **Note**   FD Feedburner‡ – This WP plug-in forwards all feed traffic transparently to Feedburner.

Be sure to make the content previews (snippets) in your RSS feed compelling to encourage more readers to click through and read the full entry. This will get you more return visitors than just using the default option of including the first couple of sentences in the post as the snippet.

RSS feeds have two additional usages. First, you can display feeds from other sites on your own. This ensures that your site is kept fresh with current content. However, if your site already has unique content, you can take advantage of the other usage. You can do the opposite and release content from your site as feeds that other sites may use. The benefit of this is that your feed includes embedded links back to your site which are under your control, providing you with a piece of their site's traffic. The willingness of others to use such feeds as content for their sites will depend on how useful and relevant it is to them. You can promote your feed on RSS directories, such as Feedage.§

Email Newsletters

Another way to keep your visitors informed and returning to your website is by publishing an email newsletter. Newsletters tend to attract more subscribers and traffic than RSS feeds, mainly because they are easier to use and feel more personal. How often you send out the email depends on how often you release new content. A weekly newsletter is usually the best choice. A daily email may be too much and a monthly too little.

---

*http://www.google.com/webmasters/add.html
†http://feedburner.google.com
‡http://wordpress.org/plugins/feedburner-plugin/
§http://www.feedage.com

Begin by creating a legitimate email list by asking your visitors to sign up for the service on your site. Once you have started gathering an email list you need email content to send out. There are two ways of creating this content—automatically or manually. The automatic way is to have your RSS feed sent out as a newsletter for you, using for example Feedburner's email service. The other way is to put together the newsletter manually. This allows you to maximize its impact and usefulness, although it requires some time and effort. Be sure to include an unsubscribe option in your newsletter.

⬚ **Note**   Alo Easymail[*] – This WP plug-in allows you to compile and send out newsletters as well as to accept and manage subscriptions and unsubscriptions.

Social Networks

A third subscription method is to allow visitors to follow your site updates on social networks. You just need to include a link to your site's profile page on, for example, Facebook or Twitter. A person already participating in the same social network may be more likely to subscribe using this option rather than using RSS feeds or newsletters.

Encouraging Subscribers

There are many ways of increasing the percentage of visitors that subscribe to your site. One way is of course to include multiple subscription alternatives—RSS, newsletters, and social networks. Another is to make sure that signing up for a subscription is easy and contains as few steps as possible.

You want to make your subscription buttons prominent without being annoying. A good idea is to place one set of links above the fold in your menu or sidebar, and a second set below the content. You may even want to spell out the invitation somewhere to further increase the percentage of visitors that sign up. For example, a simple "Enjoyed this post? Get more like it by following us on Twitter" can be placed below the content. Another tip for encouraging visitors to subscribe is to offer an incentive for doing so, such as a free download of something with high perceived value.

---

*http://wordpress.org/plugins/alo-easymail/

CHAPTER 33

Sales Pages

Third Page Type

The third page type is the sales page. The purpose of a sales page is to convert a visitor into a paying customer. This process is called a conversion. Each sales page should be product specific. That is, it should be dedicated to a single product or offer.

Sales Page Content

An effective sales page will typically contain the following items:

- **Description** – A short description of the product offered.
- **Benefits** – A bulleted list of benefits.
- **Image** – A picture or graphical representation of your product.
- **Buy button** – A clearly visible buy-now button.
- **Price** – The price of the product next to the buy button.

If you offer a guarantee, have a good testimonial, a limited special offer or have received an award for your product, then you can include those elements as well. Still, you want to keep the sales page simple with as few distractions as possible to ensure a high conversion rate.

Product Name

A good product name will help to advertise your product. The name should explain what the product is or what it can do. Make sure that it is easy to pronounce and memorable, so that people can remember it after hearing it only once. Preferably, the name should be unique so that it is not confused with any other products. You may want to use keywords in your product name that people search for when looking for answers to the problem your product helps to solve. If you can think of a name that has some or all of these attributes, this will make it easier to market your product.

The product name must appear on the product itself. The name should also appear on the title of the sales page, on its headline and in the product image.

Product Description

On the sales page, include a 100-300 word description of the product. Keep it concise and to the point. Explain clearly what the product is, what makes it special, and how it can improve the life of the buyer or solve a problem they have. Make it factual without too many hyped-up positive terms. People do not like to be sold to, so use restraint on your sales page. You want to build up a desire in the customer to buy the product without trying too hard to push the sale.

Product Benefits

Include a bulleted list of the specific benefits received from using your product. These benefits are the results the customer can expect to achieve from using your product. The list contains the promises or claims you make to the buyer of your product in order to further motivate them to buy it. It should communicate direct, specific, and immediate benefits.

Make sure the product claims are truthful or it will harm your credibility. In addition to being truthful, you also want them to be believable. People will not buy from you if they do not believe you can deliver what they expect to get. Below are some suggestions on how to enhance the believability of your product claims.

- **Specific descriptions** – You can increase your believability by converting general statements into specific descriptions. For example, instead of saying your product is "fast", describe exactly how fast it is.

- **Tone down claims** – If a claim sounds too good to be true, your customers will assume it is not true. Tone down such claims and they will be more likely to buy. When your product over-delivers they will also be more likely to recommend your product to others.

- **Odd numbers** – Avoid using round numbers in your claims. Instead, reduce them to specific odd numbers with decimals. For example, 19.7% is more believable than 20%.

- **Supporting evidence** – Make it easy to verify the accuracy of your product claims, for example, by including testimonials or by linking to third-party references that support your claims.

Product Image

Show a professional picture of your product near the description. If your product is not physical then a graphical representation of the product can be designed and used. This image is important since it will make the product appear more real, just as if it were in a physical store. It will also give customers visual confirmation that the product is in fact what they are looking for and it will even increase the perceived value of the product. Clicking the product image should display a larger image if this adds anything.

Product Purchase Button

The sales page must include a clearly visible Buy Now button above the fold. Once a visitor has decided to click through to the sales page they are already partially sold. If they cannot immediately find the purchase button they may get frustrated or reconsider the purchase. A good location for the button is just below the product image. The button should have a color, size, and design that attracts the visitor's attention.

To keep costs and administrative work low, it can be a good idea to accept orders only through your website. If people cannot telephone, fax or e-mail in an order most of them will buy on the website instead. This cost saving approach is used by, for example, Amazon.

Product Price

Next to the purchase button the price of the product should be clearly stated. Determining the starting price of your product is best done by observing what competitors charge for similar products. From that price you can later experiment both upwards and downwards to see how it affects your sales. A too high price will lower your sales. However, a low price can also be bad since your product may then be perceived as low quality. You need to find the balance in between that yields the highest net revenue. Keep in mind that odd pricing—meaning prices that end in 5's, 7's, and especially 9's—tends to sell better than rounded prices.

Informational Sales Page

Some people are motivated by long sales pages, others are not. For visitors who want additional information, you can add an informational sales page that includes these details. Add a link to this subpage from your main sales page and vice versa. On the informational sales page you can include plenty of sales copy to deal with common objections the potential customer may have and to further motivate them to buy. In addition to the more technical information, this page can include, for example, stories, examples, and video of the product usage. There may also be room for testimonials, statistics, and awards. If the page requires scrolling, be sure to include more than one purchase button.

Thank You Page

Once the order has been confirmed redirect the customer to a page thanking them for the purchase. This page can include details of when and how the product will reach the customer. If the sale was for a physical product, you can give an estimate of when the product will be arriving by mail. If it was for a digital item, you can tell them that the download link will be sent out as soon as their payment has been validated. Be sure to send the content of the Thank You page to the customer as an e-mail as well. This will give the customer immediate feedback that the order has been received.

Another important purpose of the Thank You page is to track your conversion rate. This can be done by setting a conversion goal* from Google Analytics. When specifying the goal of reaching the Thank You page, you should also define the goal funnel. These are the pages that lead up to the Thank You page, such as the sales page and any checkout pages. By specifying these, you will be able to see where visitors may drop off while on the path to completing the goal. Once you have set up a goal you will be able to track the results from the Conversions ➤ Goals category of your Analytics account.

Note that if you are using PayPal to handle payments you should enable the auto return† setting from your PayPal account. This way customers will be automatically sent to the specified Thank You page after a purchase has been completed.

Multiple Products

An e-commerce site that sells multiple products should include a shopping cart system. This cart is shown on all pages together with the number of items and the total price. Be sure that it remembers added items for a long period of time.

With multiple products you should take advantage of potential add-on sales. One of the easiest ways to increase sales is to let customers who are about to make a purchase know about related products they may also want to buy. Selling to your existing customers is always easier than acquiring new ones.

Note   WordPress Simple Paypal Shopping Cart‡ – This plug-in allows you to add a shopping cart to your site.

---

*https://support.google.com/analytics/answer/1032415
†https://www.paypal.com/cgi-bin/webscr?cmd=p/mer/express_return_summary-outside
‡http://wordpress.org/plugins/wordpress-simple-paypal-shopping-cart/

Make it Easy to Order

The customer should not have to work really hard to buy something. If you make the purchase easier, a greater percentage of visitors will buy your product.

- **Few decisions** – You should ask for as few decisions as possible. If you need to ask the user to make a decision, all the necessary information needs to be supplied to make it an easy decision.

- **Minimizing steps** – You want to minimize the number of steps necessary to complete an order.

- **Easy to revert** – Reverting a choice should be easy. Make sure the fields will remain filled out if the visitor moves backwards in the order process.

- **Do not ask for too much** – The less you ask for the more likely the customer is to follow through with the purchase. Ask for the minimum amount of information you need to complete the transaction. Do not force visitors to register before they can make a purchase.

When selling via PayPal you may not have to ask for any information at all. You can obtain the address, name, and almost anything else you may need to know about the customer from their PayPal account. These details can be sent to your server automatically by PayPal whenever a purchase is made through an *Instant Payment Notification* (IPN).*

Automated Payment System

The payment and delivery system must be automated as much as possible to make it scalable and to free up your time. The steps for complete automation are outlined below.

1. The purchase button on your sales page takes the customer to a secure payment site, such as PayPal, where they pay for your product.

2. PayPal sends out an IPN to a specified script on your server. This notification includes information regarding the customer and the transaction status.

3. The script verifies the details of the transaction and takes necessary actions. If the payment has completed, the script sends out an e-mail.

---

*https://www.paypal.com/ipn

Depending on what you sell, the e-mail sent out can be one of the following:

- **Digital product** – A temporary download link. Alternatively, you can include the digital product as an e-mail attachment if it is not too large.

- **Physical product** – A filled out order form to your distributor.

- **Automated service** – An activation link or a confirmation that the service has been activated.

For digital products a complete automation can be achieved fairly easily using the following plug-in.

◼ **Note**   Cashie Commerce* – This is a WP plug-in for selling products through PayPal.

Be sure to test your automated payment system extensively before making it live. For this purpose, PayPal has a Sandbox version† that allows you to perform tests without having to use real money.

Conversion Rate Optimization and Tracking

Once you have created a quality product or automated service, and have started to earn some money from it, you can begin the process of optimizing your conversion rate. The conversion rate is the percentage of your visitors who perform a desirable action, such as buying a product or signing up for a service. Conversion Rate Optimization (CRO) involves changing and repositioning elements on the sales page to increase the conversion rate.

Measuring and testing are the keys to improving your conversion rate. It is very difficult to predict how a change will impact your conversion rate without testing it. To effectively test variations of different page elements on your sales page you can use Google Analytics. Under the Content ➤ Experiments page, you can set up testing to determine which version of a page has the highest conversion rate.

You can, for example, test different headlines, product descriptions, product benefits, offers, graphical content or payment buttons. You may also want to vary the number of elements on the page and test different positions for the elements, in order to find the layout that brings you the greatest conversion rate.

Once the experiment is set up you only need to wait for enough sales to be made so that you can draw conclusions as to which combination of page elements performs the best. If you do not have a lot of visitors you can speed up the experiment by running a PPC campaign and sending the prospects directly to your sales page.

---

*http://wordpress.org/plugins/cashie-commerce/
†https://developer.paypal.com

CHAPTER 34

Credibility

Credibility is one of the most critical factors affecting your online business success. Before anyone will buy from you, your website or company needs to be seen as credible. This means that consumers can purchase from you and not worry about the safety of their credit card or personal information. It also means that they trust that your product will do everything you claim it will.

Being credible is simply the perception of being trustworthy and believable. While this is important for any type of website, it is especially so for e-commerce sites. It takes much more to get people to trust in your sales page's product claims than to trust what is written on a content page.

Credibility Indicators

Acquiring the visitor's trust is not that difficult. It is just a matter of presenting a professional online image. The most powerful credibility builder is a high quality website. Some of the keys to a high quality website that have been discussed already are:

1. **Professional design** – Project a high level of professionalism through your site design.

2. **Usability** – Make it easy to use and navigate your site.

3. **Consistency** – Aim for a consistent page design, writing style, and product quality.

4. **Efficiency** – Provide fast downloads, page response times, email responses and delivery time.

5. **Lack of errors** – Make sure your site code is error free and that your content is spell checked.

6. **Useful** – Providing free and useful information will by extension make your products seem more reliable.

7. **Frequent updates** – People assign more credibility to sites that show they have been recently updated or reviewed.

8. **Brand** – A brand represents a level of quality that customers may recognize and trust.

Secure Ordering

Your e-commerce website must offer secure online ordering. If you are processing your customers' orders online, you need to place the order from a secure server. This will protect your customers' personal information and give your customers added confidence in placing an order with you. In addition, make sure to let your visitors know that their information will be securely processed. You may also want to register for a security provider, such as VeriSign or Trust-e, and display their logo prominently.

Alternatively, you can let PayPal or similar companies handle your customers' payments. Through this method you will make use of PayPal's credibility, so your site will need less trust for the buy. The customer will feel safer to make the purchase since they know your website will never see their credit card number.

Guarantees

A strong guarantee will provide your visitor with greater confidence to purchase your product. Try to make your guarantee simple and without too many conditions. Always honor your guarantee without question or delay and with complete professionalism.

Guarantees can do three things: increase sales, enhance value and reduce returns. They increase sales because they reduce the risks associated with the purchase. The stronger the guarantee the larger the increase of sales. Secondly, guarantees enhance the perceived value of the product by showing that you are willing to stand by your product claims. The third thing guarantees will do is to reduce returns since they make the customer feel more comfortable with their purchase.

The guarantee will not cause you to lose money. People very rarely go to the trouble of returning items they have purchased. You will only have to reimburse a few people, but you will have many more ordering from you as a result of the guarantee. Here are some examples of guarantees:

- **Money back guarantee** – If the customer regrets their purchase, allow them to send it back for a full refund within a period of time. The standard is 30 days, but the longer the guarantee is the fewer refunds you will typically receive.

- **Low price guarantee** – If a customer buys from you and then finds the product at a lower price elsewhere, offer to refund them the difference.

- **Lifetime guarantee** – If the product is not working properly, let the customer send it back for repair free of charge.

- **Upgrade guarantee** – If a new version of your product is released within a period after a customer's purchase, offer to upgrade theirs for free.

Testimonials

A testimonial is a statement from a happy customer saying how your product has helped them. They can be a powerful way to generate trust and thus increase sales, because they provide evidence that you have already delivered what you promise to other customers. Be sure to include your customer's name and location with each testimonial to increase its believability. Another good idea is to post real pictures of your happy customers next to their testimonials.

Getting Testimonials

If you have an excellent product, the chances are high that some of your customers have already sent you positive comments which you can use for your testimonials. If not, there are ways to elicit such feedback. One effective technique is to run a customer feedback survey. In this survey, encourage your customers to describe how your product has helped them in their own words. The survey can also be used to collect other valuable data, such as suggestions on how to improve your product.

After you have run your survey and found some positive comments, ask those customers for permission to publish them. It is great if they allow their full name, location, and even a picture of themselves to be published along with their comment, as that increases the testimonials' believability. If they shy away from this, however, ask to just publish their comment together with, for example, their first name and last initial.

Never make up testimonials to enhance your credibility, as you may be caught out and discredited. If nobody will give you positive feedback, something is wrong with your product. Improve it and try again.

Where to Use Testimonials

Take the time to compile the positive feedback received into a customer testimonials page on your site. This page should be linked to from each of your sales pages. Prominently display a few of your best testimonials on your sales pages and even on your front page. Another great place to use testimonials is in areas of your site that are common abandonment points, such as checkout and shipping pages.

If you have gathered quite a few testimonials, you will probably have a different comment to suit all the major sales pages on your site. Use those that are the most convincing to potential customers. The most effective testimonials are those that describe a specific result your customer has enjoyed by using your product.

CHAPTER 35

Credibility Pages

Fourth Page Type

The fourth type of web pages—*credibility pages*—relate to those that enhance your site's credibility in some way. They are especially important for e-commerce sites.

About Page

The About page allows you to tell the story behind your site and thereby make a connection with the visitors who want to know more about it. This page also provides another way of showing that your site is a legitimate web business that they can trust.

Below is a checklist of items that you can display on your About page to reinforce your credibility. Note that the About page can include several subpages.

- A brief description and history of your site or company.

- Your website or company objectives.

- Professional photos and descriptions of yourself or the company members.

- A personal or professional biography.

Contact Page

Including a clearly visible page with a contact form allows users to send a message to the site owner on the site itself. This form of communication is better than an email link since it appears more professional and does not leave your email address available for email spam crawlers to collect. Furthermore, a contact form provides a more immediate means of communicating than having to open an emailing application to send the message. To make it as simple as possible for visitors to contact you, make sure not to include any unnecessary forms. Their email address, subject, and message are often enough.

Your Contact page should include your contact information. Providing this information will make visitors more comfortable because your business will be perceived as being more legitimate. The visitors want to at least know the name and physical address of you or your company.

If you get a lot of e-mail messages, you can hire a company to handle them for you. Make sure that the person who answers the email is knowledgeable in the site's niche and can communicate with grace and style. Also be sure that the email is answered within 24 hours. Efficient business procedures that are focused on providing customer satisfaction will enhance your site's credibility.

⬛ **Note**   Fast Secure Contact Form* – This WP plug-in adds a customizable contact form to your site.

FAQ Page

Often, visitors will have questions about your products and services. To reduce the number of these inquires you receive, be sure to include a page that answers the most common of these questions. This will enhance your site's credibility because it shows that you care about answering people's questions regarding your product. It also shows that you actually have customers, which is very important for the image of an e-commerce site. Going one step further, you can create a support forum, in which customers may help to answer their own questions.

Privacy Policy Page

When asking visitors to provide private information—such as their name, email, or credit card number—you need to display a link to your privacy policy page. On this page you tell the visitor exactly how you will be using the information you collect. There are a number of generators that can help you create a privacy policy specific to your website—for example, the OECD Privacy Statement Generator.[†]

404 Page

A custom 404 (file not found) page can help you retain more traffic and will appear more professional than the server's default 404 page. Make sure it includes your standard site template and navigation in addition to informing the visitor that they have found the page in error. Avoid placing the actual term "404" on the page.

⬛ **Note**   Permalink Finder[‡] – This WP plug-in helps visitors find what they were looking for when encountering a 404 error.

---

*http://wordpress.org/plugins/si-contact-form/
†http://www.oecd.org/sti/privacygenerator
‡http://wordpress.org/plugins/permalink-finder/

PART 6

Conclusion

▓ ▓ ▓

CHAPTER 36

Action Steps

Congratulations on reaching the last chapter of this book. At this point, you have a solid understanding of what you need to do to create an income generating website. Moreover, you understand more about how to earn money online than most people trying to make a living on the net. Now it is time to put that to use.

This chapter contains a short overview of the steps involved in creating a passive income generating site. Each step is also a milestone that you can use to measure your progress towards your passive income goal. So here they are—the seven steps to building an income generating website:

1. Preparation

2. Site setup

3. Site design

4. Content generation

5. Monetization strategies

6. Marketing

7. Repetition

The skill sets required to build a profitable website are substantial. You should know that you do not need to learn every aspect yourself in order to be successful. Any step can be delegated. You can, for example, hire help from Freelancer[1] or Elance.[2] If you need ongoing help you can take advantage of a virtual assistance firm, such as AskSunday[3] or Brickwork India.[4] Keep in mind, though, that knowing the skills of a web entrepreneur will give you a stronger bargaining position when hiring professionals. You will also be able to tell if their performance is worth their salary.

---

[1]http://www.freelancer.com
[2]http://www.elance.com
[3]http://www.asksunday.com
[4]http://www.brickworkindia.com

Preparation

Before you start building a site, you need to choose what type of site you want to build—informational, entertaining or e-commerce. You also need to decide upon a niche and how you will earn money within that niche. Additionally, you should write a business plan for the site that outlines the goals you have for it and the steps you need to take to achieve them.

Site Setup

The next step is to set up your site. You register with a hosting company to get a web server. You then choose a suitable available domain name that you register and forward to your server. On your server you install and configure WordPress,[5] along with any plug-ins you plan on using. By this stage you now have your own website up and running on your own server with your own domain name.

Site Design

From the WordPress theme directory,[6] choose an elegant and well-coded template that closely fits your purposes. Rework the design and layout as necessary. Then optimize the site for high search engine rankings and to load quickly. Check browser compatibility and make sure that it validates correctly. Also make sure the site has good navigation and usability. When you are satisfied with the results, make your website live and move on to the next step.

Content Generation

In order to attract and keep visitors, your site needs content. Perform a keyword research to discover what content people search for within your niche. Use this information to create high quality keyword specific content pages. For each content page you create, make sure to keyword optimize it and to make it sticky.

Monetization Strategies

Add multiple streams of income to your site. Remember the five ways of making money from a site: donations, advertising, affiliates, services, and products. Use the ones that fit your site best. Optimize the conversion rate by improving your sales pages and by adding credibility indicators to your site. Each monetization strategy you add, and conversion rate optimization you apply, will raise the income you receive per visitor.

---

[5]http://codex.wordpress.org/Installing_WordPress
[6]http://wordpress.org/themes/

Marketing

When you have a way of earning money from your site, and it contains value in the form of content, it is time to start actively promoting it. Use link building strategies to acquire quality back links from relevant high ranking sites. The process of increasing your site traffic is seldom a fast one. To speed things up you can launch a PPC campaign as well, provided that you have a significant enough income per visitor.

Repetition

At this stage you have three areas to work on for increasing your income: marketing, content, and monetization strategies. Determine your weakest area and focus your efforts there. Again, to recap:

- **Marketing** – Brings traffic to your site through the creation of quality back links.

- **Content** – Keeps traffic at your site. High quality content makes visitors stay longer and come back often. It also attracts traffic and establishes credibility.

- **Monetization** – Improves your income per visitor.

Work on the area that you deem will give you the biggest return on time invested. Continue this process until you reach your income goal or go on to create another site.

Multiple Sites

Once your first site has started to grow, you want to consider building your next one. Running multiple sites has many benefits in terms of income generation.

- **Learning** – It brings down the learning curve drastically for the online money making game. You can try out different marketing, content and monetization strategies on different sites and apply what works across all sites in your portfolio.

- **Diversify** – It gives you multiple diversified streams of income. If one stream goes down, the chances are another will go up.

- **Experiment** – It lets you experiment with different niches, site types and content types – some of which will be more profitable than others.

- **Time** – Traffic for a high quality site tends to grow naturally over time. The more sites you have the more you will benefit from this.

- **Leverage** – You can use your sites to market your other sites. By sharing your visitors, you can multiply your profits.

I recommend that you take the path of building more than one website. There are few individuals who can make a living from a single website. Those who can almost always have several sites worth of experience behind them, or invest a great deal of time in maintaining their site's success.

Web Entrepreneurship

If you want to earn a passive income from your online efforts to support your lifestyle without an ordinary job, you need to think of yourself as a web entrepreneur. As a web entrepreneur, your role is not one of continual content generation or web marketing. It is one of creating income generating websites. That is the one goal you need to focus on. All other activities are only the means to this end.

To achieve this goal, you want to focus on building low maintenance or completely maintenance-free sites—fully automatic systems that generate money. For this to work, automation is key. Recurring tasks that cannot be automated you need to delegate. You want to focus on the system and delegate the details. You may need to employ one or several people to take care of these details while you focus on the system. Tasks that you can delegate include, for example, marketing, content generation, web development and email answering.

When you are just starting out, I recommend that you do most things on your own to learn how to play the game. However, once you know that, you want to delegate more and more to free up your time for more important tasks. As a web entrepreneur, you want to decrease the amount of work you perform while your revenue increases. You are the website owner, not necessarily the person running the website or creating content for it. The goal is for your income to be completely independent from your time.

Conclusion

There you have it—the online money making game in a nutshell. The question now is, what will you do with it? When you put this book down, you have two choices. You can either let this information stay in your mind until it fades and is forgotten, or you can take action and apply it to build your own web business. If you think you will decide later, you are fooling yourself, because failing to choose is also a choice. If you do not decide to act right now, you have already decided to let things stay the way they are.

Do not let yourself get stuck in theory and learning. The real value only comes from application. If you are truly committed to creating an online business then here is what you should do next. Go through each chapter of this book one at a time and start taking action. If you find something that you cannot do right away, then highlight the idea in the margin for you to come back to later. Use the seven milestones listed at the beginning of this chapter to keep track of where you are and what you need to focus on doing. Work on building your web business consistently, a little bit each day, and you will soon begin to see results.

Good luck.

Index

www.ingramcontent.com/pod-product-compliance
Lightning Source LLC
Chambersburg PA
CBHW051239050326
40689CB00007B/1000